Bonnie and Her 21 Children

A memoir by her long-suffering husband

Fred Cappuccino JBS*

*Just Barely Surviving

Fred Cappuccino

BONNIE BOOKS INC.

ISBN 978-0-9948921-1-9

Library and Archives Canada Cataloguing in Publication
Cappuccino, Fred, 1926-, author
        Bonnie and her 21 children : a memoir by her long-suffering husband Fred Cappuccino * JBS.
ISBN 978-0-9948921-0-2 (paperback)
        1. Intercountry adoption. 2. Adoption. 3. Child welfare. 4. Racially mixed families--Ontario. 5. Cappuccino, Bonnie. 6. Cappuccino, Fred, 1926-. 7. Cappuccino family. 8. Child Haven International. I. Title.
HV875.5.C36 2016   362.734089   C2015-907371-5

www.BonnieAndHer21Children.com

Contents

Accolades and Trumpets

"I had the privilege of meeting Bonnie & Fred Cappuccino over 20 years ago when I spent time volunteering with one of their Child Haven orphanages in India. That experience changed my life, as the Child Haven organization has done for thousands of children, staff, and supporters around the world. Bonnie & Fred have lit a lamp for the whole world to see, and it will continue to glow well beyond all of our lifetimes."

Shilpi Somaya Gowda, author of Secret Daughter and The Golden Son

"I still get weak in the knees when I look at her" is Fred Cappuccino's only answer. There is no other explanation for how an idealistic Midwestern farm girl training to be a nurse and her husband, a kind-hearted, protest-prone minister from backwater Scranton, Pennsylvania, became the parents of a family that looks like the United Nations. You will chuckle your way through the amazing adventure described in *Bonnie and Her 21 Children*; that is, until you have to put the book down because you're laughing so hard you can't catch your breath or your heart has been broken and your eyes are brimming with tears. In a world too often filled with strife between countries and ethnic groups, this story shows that it is possible for the most disparate of peoples to live not just in harmony but with joy. If you want to see what love in action can do, read it. It will fill you with hope.

The Rev Dr Mark Morrison-Reed, author of many books, including *In Between: Memoir of an Integration Baby*. Also, *The Selma Awakening: How The Civil Rights Movement Tested and changed Unitarian Universalism*. Mark is a former President of the Canadian Unitarian Council and former President of the Family Service Association of Metro Toronto that delivers service in 24 languages.

This is more than a good news story about the rescue of children, including the bringing to Canada of 15 babies from war-torn Bangladesh. It's the story of two remarkable Canadians, my former neighbours in

Glengarry County, Ontario who, more than anything else, wanted to devote their lives to providing a loving home for orphans and unwanted children. Inspired by the philosophy of Mahatma Gandhi, Fred and Bonnie Cappuccino were not content to sire two and adopt nineteen children from many different racial and ethnic backgrounds, which made our county school feel like an international house. From their 170-year-old log house, they set out to prove that working, living and socializing together fosters peace and understanding. Join Fred in post-war Japan or on the front-lines in Selma, Alabama, and Bonnie organizing non-religious orphanages in India, Bangladesh, Nepal and Tibet.

I know no Canadians who have done more for the world with so little fanfare and so much grace. Like the unassuming Jean Vanier, they have earned the love and admiration of thousands, as well as the Order of Canada, the attention of CBC's "Man Alive" and CTV's "W5." Their story, which Fred tells with refreshing humour and understatement, is a story we need to hear, especially during these tumultuous and troubled times, when politicians in league with corporate elites have done so little to inspire and so much to harm. If you want something to feel good about, read this book and share it with your friends. You'll be itching to read the sequel, which tells of their founding of *Child Haven International.*

Gary Geddes, author of *What Does A House Want?* and *Drink the Bitter Root*: A writer's search for justice and healing in Africa and recipient of the Lt.-Governor's Award for Literary Excellence.

Dedication

Kailash Shantidas Tagore Cappuccino,
11 October 1973 – 21 April 1995

Whatever you make with your hands, be it a bird house or a chair, or whatever, take time to make it beautiful. - Shantidas

The butterfly counts not months but moments and has time enough – Tagore

Kailash would surely be living today if society was accepting of all people regardless of whom they love.

Mahatma Gandhi

"Ye have heard that it hath been said, Thou shalt love thy neighbour, and hate thine enemy. But I say unto you, Love your enemies, bless them that curse you, do good to them that hate you, and pray for them which despitefully use you, and persecute you..." [1]

When the young Mahatma Gandhi read these words of Jesus, he was moved to tears. This concept of non-violent love of Jesus and Gandhi formed the basis of Martin Luther King's movement for social justice.

Gandhi demonstrated on a mass scale what Jesus demonstrated on an individual scale – that love can profoundly change people for the better. Today, while many in India accord him lip-service, he has been largely forgotten in his homeland, except for groups of highly dedicated followers here and there.

When I was a university student, my first introduction to Gandhi was seeing a photograph of his possessions when he died: Indoor sandals, outdoor sandals, a bowl, a robe, and perhaps a dozen other items. That was it. Gandhi was incorruptible. He would not accept any gifts from anyone. One exception I heard of was a newly designed toilet. He accepted this to give publicity to an ongoing need in India.

I was curious to learn more, and read some 20 books about him.

Bonnie and I consider ourselves Gandhians, not in the sense of being any kind of experts – but in the sense of being committed students of his way of life. What Gandhi accomplished is impressive:

- Independence for India by non-violent means – with immediate friendly relations between Britain and India - unique in the history of the world
- A massive attack against the injustices of the caste system
- A climate of tolerance and co-existence among the various religions
- A recognition of the equal importance of women and men.

---

[1] Matthew 5:43-44, King James Version

Author's Note

97 photos have been sprinkled on this text by helicopter. 88.32% of them are in the right place. The rest are not. Please ignore the ones that are not.

Bonnie McClung Cappuccino, to whom I have been married lo these sixty plus years, is exceedingly focussed. She doesn't like to waste a minute. When she stops at a red light, she takes the opportunity to DO stuff, like rooting down into her purse. She does not look at the light. One day I said, "Bonnie - you're supposed to watch for the green arrow!"

She paused, looked at me, and, taking her time, said, "Relax, Fred. There is always some kind gentleman who will beep to let me know the light has changed."

Bonnie Laura McClung had her own agenda

**Bonnie in 1945 with brothers David and Bruce, who testify that
she bossed them around too**

The account of this erudite and entertaining book covers 1953-2004, roughly from our marriage up to the time when the last of the children left home - and Bonnie ran out of steam regarding adopting more children into our family.

Bonnie thinks of the following as mentors, with the percentage of their relative influence on her:

Laura Mueller McClung (mother): 30%
Hugo Mueller (grandfather): 20%
Aung San Suu Kyi: 20%
Arundhati Roy: 20%
Vandana Shiva: 20%
Mahatma Gandhi: 30%
Jesus of Nazareth: 30%
The Dalai Lama: 30%
Dr S V Mapuskar: 20%
Swami Agnivesh: 20%
Dorothy Day: 30%
All of her 21 Children: 21%
Her Husband: ½ of 1% most of the time.

Bonnie doesn't add very well. That's how she wound up with 21 children instead of our agreed-upon four.

Bonnie and Her 21 Children [2]

[2] This book is 96.7 % true.

Chapter 1

Out of the Shambles, I Find Her

All through university my love life had been a shambles. I would meet a girl, get to know her, and entrust my quivering heart to her. Then I would say or do something stupid - and I'd get the axe. Some weeks or months later, I would find another girl, and entrust my battered and quivering heart to her. Then I would say or do something stupid - and I'd get the axe. This happened over and over and over.

With my life at a low ebb anyhow, it was a good time for an experiment. Mahatma Gandhi had said, *Whatever possessions you own that you don't really need - are a theft from the poor.* Pondering this truism, I decided to cull my possessions. I got rid of lots of clothes, books, paper clips, and my aloe vera plant. I kept my portable typewriter, some bedding, and some clothes plus 75 books, winnowed down from 300. I was down to 150 pounds of belongings. Then, gradually, stuff accumulated again.

At the Garrett Theological Seminary, a Methodist school in Evanston, Illinois, a new semester started. My morale was low. Joanie, a student nurse, had just given me the axe in favour of a more sensible theolog. I had lent Joanie my copy of Dorothy Baruch's book, *One Little Boy* a psychological study.

On a sunny Sunday afternoon in January, 1953, five student nurses (sans Joanie) walked the cold mile from their Nurse's Residence to return the book to me. It had apparently made the rounds of their dormitory. The five young women entered the arched vestibule-parlour at the Seminary, and asked for me. One of my buddies hollered down the steps: *"Hey, Cappuccino! Put yer pants on! - five female girls of the opposite sex to see you! -*

five of them!" I was, of course, electrified. I composed myself, swallowed what I was chewing, leapt up the stairs, and sauntered coolly into the parlour to face this collective cluster of comeliness. One avails oneself of the opportunity to extend a right hand, to take each soft and gentle hand, and leisurely introduce oneself to each of these delicious morsels.

Of the five, only one name do I remember: the exotic appellation - "Bonnie McClung." She had a mesmerizing smile. Something about the name stirred my sleeping half-Celtic blood. I thanked them all for bringing the book and they left. That very afternoon I girded up my courage and phoned the Nurses' Residence and asked for Bonnie McClung. She came to the phone and said, "Hello."

"Hi, Bonnie, this is Fred Cappuccino. I saw you at Garrett this morning."

"Yes, it was good to meet you."

"I was wondering if I could come over and see you."

"That would be fine."

This was too good to be true. Reluctant to be too pushy, I nevertheless ventured, "When?"

"How about 7 o'clock this evening?"

"Great! - see you then!" I was elated, euphoric, exhilarated, not to mention, ecstatic.

I have since learned that Bonnie doesn't waste time. I was being drawn into a typhoon vortex that was to dizzify me for the rest of my life. I was chronically broke. That didn't matter to her; she was broke, too. We courted along the waterway, imaginatively yclept by some Illinois politician:

the Sanitary District Canal.

We often walked past the glorious Baha'i Temple, looking benevolently down upon us from the other side. Sometimes we took the EL train down into Chicago for free entertainment at "Bughouse Square," where the government allowed unhindered free speech. In one corner a communist harangued four listeners about the class struggle; in another corner a libertarian opined loudly that we should have more freedom in our lifestyle. A stout woman in her 60s delivered a "lecture on sex." "Sex," she shouted, "is sacred. It is too important a matter to be traded for money. And don't believe what anyone may have told you. The gospel truth is that I never, ever, gave sex for money." She was roundly applauded.

Each evening, as we strolled by the canal, our discussion often centred on a future in which children were a common theme. Bonnie wanted to help save the children of the world. She told me she could not worship a vengeful God. That was even before she became an Agnostic. Even back then the image of little children across the seas, or anywhere, holding up begging bowls, was real to the two of us. Why wasn't it real to everyone? Too soon, time ran out and we hurried back to the Nurses' Residence, arriving right on the deadline, just before the guardian of the girls' collective morals was bolting the door to contain virtue inside and exclude sin outside. Sin made his thoughtful way back to Garrett.

I had been taking her a flower every day now that the snow was gone. Sometimes a tiny blossom from a hedge. Once a surreptitiously swiped red tulip from the park. I brought her a different kind of flower each time. Bonnie says they are all pressed into a book somewhere.

Our joint activities included meetings of the new Evanston Chapter of the Congress of Racial Equality (CORE), a vibrant, inter-racial group, mostly students. For a while I had the good fortune to chair the boisterous weekly meetings. Humour abounded. Whenever a new person was introduced at the meeting, we'd go around and tell our names. One deep-voiced fellow routinely introduced himself as "God." He wasn't.

We tested restaurants in Evanston. A well-dressed Black couple would go to a restaurant to see if they would be admitted. A white couple would follow. If the Black couple were turned away - "No tables left," or some other excuse - and the white couple was then admitted, the restaurant probably had a biased policy. While Evanston had a problem with segregated housing and recreational facilities, the restaurants seemed to be open. Good thing, because we paid for the dinners ourselves, and couldn't afford a lot of testing.

Incidentally, Bonnie claims that on her father's side, her great grandmother was perhaps part Native American Indian. Her father was proud of that, but some of his 12 siblings were adamant that Grandma Brown was too refined to be part Native Indian. They were raised that way in the Deep South. Bonnie felt sorry for them. She claims one 32nd part Native Indian heritage.

Bonnie knew where she was going long before I came into her life. She planned to finish nurses' training, remain in nursing, and work her way through university. After that other doors would open and she would find a way to work with small children in the slums of Chicago. That was her plan.

I asked her to marry me, and I even promised her father that I would make sure she finished her university education. But events precluded that as we shall see. I asked her what kind of engagement ring she wanted. She said, "What I would *really* like is a mustard seed pendant." [3] She knew I was a penniless theolog. It cost me five bucks. She treasured it. Our first baby teethed on it.

At the seminary it was the custom to announce wedding engagements at the evening meal in the cafeteria. During the announcement time a friend would get up and pretend to make a routine announcement, saying something like, "There is going to be a meeting of the blah blah society next Tuesday at 7:30, and blah blah blah, and by the way, Jack and Susan are now engaged." The crowd would cheer and make a big fuss. Bonnie often came as a guest, and wondered when I would ask a friend to announce our engagement. I was hesitating because I felt guilty, as she was so young.

---

[3] Matthew 17:20: "for verily I say unto you, If ye have faith as a grain of mustard seed, ye will say unto this mountain, Remove hence to yonder place; and it shall remove; and nothing shall be impossible unto you."

But she would have none of that. She said, "Well, don't bother to see me any more until you decide whether or not to announce it." As I was walking home that evening I was smiling. Her "taking a stand" appealed to me.

When I did or said something stupid, she would cut her hair shorter because she knew I liked her long hair. I worried that by the time we married she would be bald. I had just been ordained after finishing seminary. Before the wedding, full of idealism, we asked our Methodist bishop to send us to a difficult Charge. He did. Chicago's McKinley Park Methodist Church on Chicago's southwest side had kicked out its three previous ministers. I was sent there in June, 1953, and lived alone in the parsonage next door. Bonnie came to hear my lousy sermons, but lived at her parents' home in Palatine, 50 miles away. In those days no hanky panky for unmarrieds.

We wanted to invite my Black roommate from Garrett Seminary to be Best Man. Bonnie's brothers got wind of this and said, "If you invite a Black person we won't come to the wedding, and Dad (who was raised in the South) won't either." Bonnie and I agonized over this and finally decided that a wedding is a family affair. We did not invite him. Luckily he didn't know about all this. Advocacy would come later.

We planned a small discrete wedding in July with just a few friends. Bonnie's mother said, "Not for *MY* daughter!" After entreating, pleading, and imploring on bended knee, we realized there was no non-violent way of holding her back. We finally capitulated to a formal church wedding, with five gowns, five monkey suits, and a reception with scores of relatives and friends. Bonnie was 19, I was 27, and full of guilt for "robbing the cradle."

Bonnie and Fred wedding, July, 1953

But actually, it was not all that extravagant. At our wedding reception in the Methodist Church in Dundee, Illinois, a simple buffet of sandwiches and dessert was served by the Women's Society. No going into debt as many families do, especially in India, where ordinary families invite hundreds of people to the wedding and full dinner.

Why did I marry her? First, her drop-dead gorgeous countenance. Second, the everlasting broad smile on her face. Third, her predilection for mayhem. She is up for anything. Of any hare-brained idea of mine suggested half in jest, she'll say, "Let's try it." Also, she never gave me the axe, although she really pinched me hard a few times.

We decided to have two children born to us - in keeping with Zero Population Growth - and if she wanted more, to adopt one or two. But she gets carried away. She knows I'm totally enchanted with her and she takes advantage. I was naively unaware that she was afflicted with an incurable ailment: "Cerebrum Infanti," some kind of Latin for "Babies on the Brain."

The church paid a munificent $2500 per annum, but better yet, had a parsonage next door. No furniture, to be sure, but *all that room*. Bonnie thought of all the children she could fit into those *five rooms* (including bath). Sudden affluence.

Parsonage with our 1940 Packard

After some weeks of marriage, I hinted to Bonnie that I would really enjoy some of her glorious apple pie. She said, "Well, you found fault with the last pie I made, so I'm not making any more."

Insulted and bruised, I countered, "OK, if you're going to be that way, I'll make my own." Bonnie smiled a malevolent smile.

I got out the recipe book, the flour, the Crisco, the sugar, the apples, pans, etc., etc. The aggregation covered the entire kitchen table. After several hours of false starts and cleaning up various spills, I finally finished and set it carefully into the oven. I sat and waited by the oven door. Bonnie amusedly offered, "Well, don't just sit there waiting, Fred, it'll take a long time."

She added, "And do your waiting in the kitchen - I don't want flour tracked all over the house."

It was a long wait. Finally the timer rang. I burned myself twice getting the pie out of the oven and onto the table. It was the most beautiful pie in the world. I got a table knife. She said, "You can't cut it now - you have to wait 'til it cools."

"How long will that take?"

"Oh, I don't know" - another broad smile - "a couple of hours."

I remembered my training in high school Physics. (I was very good in Physics). With my superior knowledge about heat and cold, I said, "I'll show you something you don't know much about. Water cools things fast."

I got the big dish pan out, and poured in three inches of cold water. I thought, if I barely touch the bottom of the hot pie pan to the cold water, it should cool quickly. I grabbed the pie with hot pads. What I forgot to remember was another law of Physics, that when a body is immersed in water, the water rises. As the pie slowly descended, the cold water rapidly ascended, and flooded over the top of my masterpiece. Bonnie, with a total lack of empathy, shrieked with laughter.

Over the sink I drained as much water off as I could, and sat down to enjoy a slice of my soggy pie. I had to keep a positive attitude (it wasn't quite what I had hoped for). As I took my second mouthful, I asked Bonnie, "Would you like some?" bringing her to a convulsion so intense that her sides ached. My soggy pie wasn't too bad. It lasted me about a week. She has been getting the better of me ever since.

The *Chicago Tribune* had a series about unwanted babies left at Cook County Hospital in Chicago. They were looking for foster families.

Bonnie applied to an agency for foster children. We had all that space, and Bonnie felt each day that went by without children was wasted. The social worker said she would come to our house on Tuesday morning.

We were expecting her at 10:30. She rang the doorbell at 10:00. The front room was in disarray. We invited her in anyhow and sat her in our one stuffed chair. I moved the vacuum cleaner off the cluttered carpet, and we sat on the apple crates and boards that were our furniture. We explained that we had lots of room as she could see, and we could borrow cribs into which to put babies. We fully expected that she would jump at the chance to let us have at least one child. After all, there were so many without homes. As she left she said she would be back in touch a week later.

We waited anxiously for a week. She returned and reported that she fully appreciated our good intentions and high degree of motivation, but her decision was that we hadn't been married long enough. Perhaps some time in the future, etc., etc. As we look back on it, perhaps three months is not enough time for a couple to get adjusted to married life. But at that time we were utterly devastated. After the worker left, Bonnie sat in my lap in the same stuffed chair and cried for a solid hour.

Chapter 2

Our First-Born – 103 Adoption Agencies

Robin Hood Cappuccino *arrived in 1954. Robin Hood was a legendary hero of 12th century England who helped the downtrodden and defenceless.*

We never again applied for foster children. They are not really "yours." The agency can take them away from you at any time.

We admired Gandhi's teachings on simple living. Gandhi had an unlikely ally in this way of thinking in U.S. President Dwight Eisenhower who, at the beginning of his presidency, said:

> *"Every gun that is made, every warship launched, every rocket fired, signifies, in the final sense, a theft from those who hunger and are not fed, those who are cold and are not clothed. This world in arms is not spending money alone. It is spending the sweat of its laborers, the genius of its scientists, the hope of its children."* [4]

Bonnie and I slept on the floor, on futon quilts as people in Japan do – no need for a bed. We rolled up the futons and had more room during the daytime. The flu flattened me one day. The local physician, Dr

---

[4] as quoted in Marian Wright Edelman, p77, *The Measure of Our Success*, Beacon Press, 1992

Turner, came for a house call. Apparently he was appalled to see me sleeping on the floor. He didn't say anything to us about it, but we heard that he raised hell with some of the church leaders. A few days afterward we were the amused recipients of a "used-but-in-good-condition" bedroom set.

My only suit of clothes became so bedraggled that our sometimes tactful congregation presented me with a new black robe to wear in the pulpit.

Bonnie had also discarded the bulk of her clothing, including that gorgeous black and gold dress she had made which won a 4H prize. [5] She felt she should keep only two dresses, both of which she made herself - "wash and wear." The everyday one was washed at night and worn the next morning, with a second dress for Sundays. All of these were made on a foot-treadle sewing machine. Later on Bonnie made me a blue suit jacket and red vest, also on a treadle machine. I wore them until they were threadbare.

Our simple living ideals crumbled when the church gave us a wedding shower. Everybody brought things, including three sets of dishes, plus two sets of glasses. It was painful to us to be given all this "stuff," but we pretended to be grateful.

I was unprepared for one method Bonnie used to get rid of things. Once, in the middle of a noisy argument with Bonnie over something long forgotten, I left abruptly and went next door to the church to work. When I returned, the kitchen floor was awash in broken dishes. She had pulled them off the pantry shelf and smashed them onto the floor. I now think twice before walking away from arguments with her, which are frequent - 3.74 times per week.

---

[5] I'm still mourning the loss of this absolutely exquisite dress. I should have insisted that she keep it.

Meanwhile a biological baby was on the way. Bonnie carried our child for a long time; it seemed like years. We would name her Annie Laurie for her two grandmothers.

After the birth Dr Turner announced: "Congratulations! Your boy has football shoulders." We needed a boy's name! A few weeks before our baby was born a newspaper reported that someone in Indiana was trying to ban the book *Robin Hood* from libraries and schools because it was "communistic." Bonnie had always liked the story of Robin Hood so we named our firstborn Robin Hood Cappuccino, born in 1954.

Robin was also named for Rabin-dranath Tagore, the poet of Bengal. When Bonnie first read his poem, "The Beginning" she was moved to tears and even unto this day she cannot read it without weeping. She wonders how this great man, continents away and a generation ago, could understand the feelings we had for each child who would join our family, whether by birth or adoption and at whatever age.

"Where have I come from, where did you pick me up?" the baby asked its mother.

She answered, half crying, half laughing, and clasping the baby to her breast, -

You were hidden in my heart as its desire, my darling. You were in the dolls of my childhood's games: and when with clay I made the image of my god every morning, I made and unmade you then.

You were enshrined with our household deity, in his worship I worshipped you.

In all my hopes and my loves, in my life, in the life of my mother you have lived.

In the lap of the deathless Spirit who rules our home you have been nursed for ages.

When in girlhood my heart was opening its petals, you hovered as a fragrance about it.

Your tender softness bloomed in my youthful limbs, like a glow in the sky before the sunrise.

Heaven's first darling, twin-born with the morning light, you have floated down the stream of the world's life, and at last you have stranded on my heart.

As I gaze on your face, mystery overwhelms me: you who belong to all have become mine.

For fear of losing you I hold you tight to my breast. What magic has snared the world's treasure in these slender arms of mine?"

As far as we know Robin has always liked his name. In fact, only one of our children disliked the name we gave him.

Puppy Elmer Fudd watching Robin Hood

All this time we were enjoying our congregation. One day some of the men had a Work Bee at the church, and farm-girl Bonnie said she'd fix lunch for them. After working all morning, they gathered at a table outside, and she served spaghetti from a huge pot. Because she was married to an Italian she wanted to make authentic Italian spaghetti, so she added a very small jar of Italian hot peppers. The men dug in. They suddenly all stopped and looked at each other. One teenager blew air out of his mouth like a blowtorch and said, "Whooooo! Anybody want some paint removed?" After we all stopped laughing, Bonnie put some sandwiches together for the rest of us, and then sat down and pretended to enjoy the spaghetti. She does like things hotter than most people.

One baby was not enough to fill Bonnie's home. With thousands of orphans at Cook County Hospital and elsewhere, she assumed it would be relatively simple to adopt a child. She wrote to the local adoption agency in Chicago, and a social worker came to visit. This time we had chairs and tables instead of boxes. During the interview we talked of many things. Perhaps we talked too much. We are, of course, passionate about racial justice. We mentioned that we would like to adopt a child who otherwise might never be adopted - a child of different racial origin or physically challenged, though we could not afford expensive surgery. The social worker said she would consider our request, although she could make no commitment whatever and didn't want to raise our hopes.

Some time later we were dumbfounded to learn that we had been refused. She said it was because we had a psychological problem: "inverted prejudice."

"What does that mean?"

"It refers to the fact that, on the one hand, you consciously decided to limit the number of children born to you. This of itself is unusual. But you also requested a mixed or minority race child. This is even more unusual, and taken together, this means that you have *inverted prejudice*. You may not realize it," she said, "but you are prejudiced against your own unborn children."

Nothing we could say would dissuade her from this judgment, not even the fact that our son, Robin, a thoroughly delightful child, was loved and cherished, and that we were planning for one more biological child.

We asked her if we could appeal this decision. She said the decision was final, and that she had talked it over with her superior "who is a Negro," and he agreed with her completely. We asked her about the children who were not adopted. Wouldn't our home be better than their having to stay in some kind of institution? She replied that all the children were well provided for, but was vague about how. For the second time in our brief marriage we were utterly crushed.

Bonnie went to the public library and found out which adoption agencies were situated within driving distance of Chicago. There were 103 agencies in five states. She wrote to all of them:

We wish to inquire about the possibility of adopting a child who is classified as "unadoptable" either because of some physical handicap or because of mixed racial background. We have one child, and are able to have more children born to us....

Two-thirds of the agencies didn't bother to answer. Those that did told us they had a strict rule that parents who were able to have children by natural means were not eligible for a child from their agency. And also couples had to have been married for five years. Then I remembered Miki Sawada, a woman I had met in Japan when I was teaching English there after the war. She had gathered some abandoned "G.I. babies" fathered by American servicemen and was raising them at her estate. We wrote to her. She sent a photograph of three little children who were adoptable, a girl five years old and two boys about six. We already had a boy, so we decided on the girl, who was Black-Japanese.

Chapter 3

Cataclysm – Adopting a Mixed-Race Child

Machiko Cappuccino *arrived in 1955. Machiko liked her name and decided to keep it.*

McKinley Park Methodist Church was in a white residential area in Chicago known for its antipathy to Blacks. One neighbourhood phenomenon was an older single woman who used to throw her neighbours into a tizzy when she threatened to "sell my house to Coloured!"

A local politician quietly let it be known that if any Blacks purchased a home in the neighbourhood, the young whites should feel free to dynamite the house, and he would see that they were not prosecuted.

Bonnie and I were determined to make a go of the church. The attendance at services increased so that the board decided to hold an additional service each Sunday to accommodate the numbers of people. The youth were passable as a choir and sang two-part harmony. When I asked them to sing at both services, one kid replied, "Rev (not "Reverend," just "Rev") we don't mind sitting through the same sermon - we don't listen to that, anyhow - but please, Rev – don't tell the same jokes twice." Morale was high. The church was growing after many lean years.

We had not told many that we planned to adopt a child from overseas. On the Sunday before our second child was to arrive, I announced to the congregation that we had adopted a little girl, five years old, through the courts in Japan by proxy, (proxy means we did not have to go to Japan), and that the child's mother was Japanese and her father was an American Negro serviceman later killed in action in Korea.

The explosion was almost literal. Some of the congregation were incensed. "We have worked for years to keep up the value and appearance of our houses, and now our nice community will be ruined!"

One lady said, "Goodbye - and I'm NOT coming back!" Ordinarily I would have been glad to hear her say that, since she was critical of every new idea. But at this point, I wondered how many others would leave, and whether there would be a congregation left. Some others left.

I wondered if my future would be similar to that of Abner in the following story: We heard of one minister who was enamoured of his own voice, and ranted so much that no congregation could stand him for very long. We'll call him the Rev. Abner Wheeler. Abner was sent to the most isolated congregation. We'll call it East Holton, where no minister wanted to go. After a year there, those poor folk told the Bishop they had taken their share of punishment, and wanted the Rev Abner Wheeler sent elsewhere. He went to another congregation, which also tired of him.

At the Annual Conference Abner had a habit of loudly proclaiming "Ah-men!" as the pastoral appointments were announced. Excitement was in the air as the District Superintendent announced: "Rev. John Jones - First Methodist Church of Swansea."

Abner intoned loudly in response: "AH-MEN!" echoing across the auditorium.

"Rev. Alex Dapper - Honesdale Charge."

Abner sang out: "AH-MEN!"

"Rev John H Smith - Waterford Charge."

Abner: "AH-MEN!"

"Rev. Abner Wheeler - East Holton Charge."

Abner: "AH - - - - SHIT!" But he went to East Holton anyhow. Names are different, but the story is true. Actually, in our present situation we would have accepted "East Holton".

The District Superintendent, Dr C Wesley Israel, was upset because I had not warned him that he might be receiving irate phone calls. Some members wanted me fired that very day. Dr Israel called me, "Why didn't you tell me you were going to do something as controversial as this, Fred, so I could be ready to respond to these people?"

I gently reminded him that I had mentioned to him some time earlier that we were intending to adopt a mixed-race child from Japan, and that he had agreed to let us use his name as a reference. He remembered, and from that point on he was supportive. His patient response to callers was, "Well, let's not get too excited - let's go easy and see how it goes with the members of the congregation. We can settle it at Quarterly Conference (the annual business meeting of the local church nine months later, at which he would preside)."

But I still had career jitters. Church law requires the Bishop to provide employment for every minister, but it doesn't say at what salary or conditions.

Meanwhile, the child would arrive in a few days at Los Angeles Airport with Mrs Miki Sawada, who was bringing eight children to adoptive homes in America.

Since joint bank account #3077-44 was depleted, a friend in the congregation lent us several hundred dollars for plane fare for me and our new daughter. Armed with the one photo of the child and a small box full of toys, crackers, and other diversions, I flew off to meet Machiko.

At Los Angeles Airport, Mrs Miki Sawada, second from left, and Machiko looking anxious with her white wicker suitcase behind her

The other new parents and I met Mrs. Sawada and the children in a reception room at the airport. There was a little girl holding a tiny wicker suitcase containing all her earthly belongings. Little hands, sad face, big brown eyes - she was even smaller than I had imagined - so fragile, so delicate. Mrs Sawada told me, "Machiko is my most intelligent child. You are very fortunate."

I approached cautiously, and told her in my very poor Japanese, [6] "I am your new father. Can you understand me?" She nodded that she understood. I was overcome with awe. What greater gift could Bonnie and I receive than this breathtakingly beautiful child - and what more terrifying responsibility.

"This doll is for you."

[6] I had spent three years in Japan earlier, working with young people

She thanked me in her quiet Japanese: *"Arigato."*

After I spoke with Mrs Sawada and sat with Machiko for some time, the party broke up and we all headed for our different return destinations in the airport. Taking Machiko's hand I walked toward the ticket counter to see about our return flight.

After a hundred feet or so it dawned on her that we were really taking leave of Mrs. Sawada, and Machiko bellowed out for all to hear that she wanted to go back to *"MAMMA-SAN! MAMMA-SAN! MAMMA-SAN!"* The sound echoed through the corridors, and everyone in the entire terminal knew I was taking a child against her will. We were obviously not blood relatives. I walked, apprehensive, dragging the screaming child along by the hand.

I was rescued by a Japan Airline employee: "You should pick her up and hold her, even if she struggles. It will be better for her." I did. She was crying less, but squirming all the while I was confirming reservations at the ticket counter. We had several hours until take-off so we went to a restaurant. When we sat on stools at the counter she understood that we were going to have something to eat and she quieted down. We each had a hamburger and a glass of milk. She handled the hamburger delicately and ate slowly. When she was finished she took her napkin and wiped the counter. Then she climbed down from the stool and wiped the seat and back of the stool with the napkin.

We arrived back home in Chicago just in time for breakfast, and Machi was welcomed by Bonnie and Robin, then 15 months old. We had eggs for breakfast. Machi hesitated to eat hers. She was saying something in Japanese and finally I was able to make out that she was hesitating because "eggs are for sick children only." I told her it was all right - she could eat her egg even though she wasn't sick. She cleaned the plate, relishing each morsel.

We had tomatoes for lunch. Bonnie cut up a large one on Machiko's plate, together with other food. She ate everything. We asked if she wanted anything else. She pointed to the tomatoes, so Bonnie gave her a second big one. Finishing that, she wanted another. She ate three large tomatoes.

One of the surprises was the relief Bonnie and I felt when Machi and Robin played together. Until she arrived, Robin had no child to play with, so he monopolized his parents' daylight hours, and a good part of the night as well. But now he and Machi would interact, and we were reprieved for *ten whole minutes* at a time.

Robin and Machiko creating masterpieces

Now that we had a girl we thought we might utilize the name, "Annie Laurie." However, Machiko was quite satisfied with the name she had. A pastor from Japan stayed with us for a few months while attending a seminary in Chicago. We asked him what "Machiko" meant. He said he would have to see it written. We fished out the adoption papers, written in Japanese, and he looked at them.

34

"Oh, your daughter has a beautiful name," he said. "It means 'watch,' in the sense that Jesus asked his disciples in Gethsemane to 'watch and wait.' It is really a beautiful, beautiful name."

The kids in the Methodist youth group were won over as soon as they met Machiko. Linda, one of the leading members of the group, lingered after a youth meeting to chat on the front steps. She said to Bonnie, "Mrs Rev, I like you and Rev - I don't care what they say." Bonnie was pleased at the compliment, but wondered, what ARE they saying?

Because of the climate against racial integration and homes being dynamited, we were sometimes apprehensive about going to sleep at night. Two weeks after Machiko's arrival, we had just gone to bed when we heard glass shattering out back. I was afraid of the possibility of fire. I peeked out through the curtains and saw some youths walking away down the alley. We waited for a long time, and there didn't seem to be any fire. We tried to get some sleep. The next morning we found they had thrown soda pop bottles against the concrete foundation of our house. We were so worried one night that we called a fellow minister a few miles away and asked to spend the night. We took our two kids and piled in with them and their five kids. It was our first good night's sleep in weeks.

When Bonnie's father heard that some church people dared to criticize his charming daughter he became a strong supporter. Machiko won over Bonnie's two brothers also who became advocates for racial justice in university.

After a few weeks church attendance levelled off at two-thirds of what it was before. We reverted back to one service on Sundays. But the contributions held firm to the previous level.

Dr Israel came and christened Machiko at a Sunday morning service. He proposed that we find out just where the congregation really stood. He suggested a vote by secret ballot be announced for a later Sunday. There was a good crowd that day. The question was clear: Write Yes or No to the question: *"I would like Rev. Cappuccino to remain as minister for the coming year."* Methodist appointments were for one year at a time. The vote was 62 Yes, 11 No.

At the Quarterly Conference sixteen leaders of the congregation gathered to meet with the District Superintendent and me. We were receiving $3200 per year by this time, and I had let it be known that I wanted a thousand dollar raise to bring my salary a little closer to the standard for my profession. The Lay Leader of the congregation said, "The Cappuccinos can stay for another year if they agree not to adopt any more controversial children." He would even support the raise we asked for. We responded that we were planning to adopt a Black-Japanese boy.

The leader said, "In that case, we request the Bishop appoint Rev. Cappuccino elsewhere and send us another minister." This leader was a lawyer who followed the seven holy habits of living: tithing, attending church, praying daily, etc.

Dr Israel said, "We have heard this one opinion expressed. Are there any other opinions?" The rest of the group were reluctant to speak because you never knew when you were going to need a lawyer's help.

Then Elsie started to weep. Elsie was a quiet amiable woman who had been church treasurer since the beginning of time. She deferred to others in the running of the church and seldom expressed an opinion. In a soft voice, but very clearly, she said, "We'll never get another couple like the Cappuccinos," and she continued weeping. Dr Israel waited for other opinions. None was forthcoming. The Quarterly Conference went on record requesting our removal at the next Annual Conference, nine months hence.

The local grocer, not a church-going type, told me, "For the life of me, I just can't understand how the church people can be so antagonistic over a small child."

One heartening development was the emergence of a vocal group in support of what we were doing. One young wife, a rough outspoken person, thought my theology left something to be desired. I had automatically pegged her as prejudiced, but she turned out to be strongly supportive and ready to say so. Other people would bring a small toy for Machiko, or some article of clothing. A few people, strangers to us, wrote letters wishing us well. These were great morale boosters.

The stares in the supermarket initially bothered us, but Bonnie's positive nature took over. She assumed goodwill on the individual's part. When a stranger asked, "Are you babysitting this child for someone?" Bonnie responded, with a big smile, "No, she's ours. Isn't she beautiful?" Usually people agreed, perhaps altering their initial impression on the spot.

We had served McKinley Park Church for three years and had received 110 new people into membership. We asked Dr Israel to send us to another difficult charge. In June we were appointed to Christ Methodist Church, about 15 miles away in Chicago.

Chapter 4

Chicago – Our Third Child

William Tell Cappuccino *arrived in 1956. William Tell was a fighter against tyranny in early Switzerland. Our son delighted in his name, and later on began using an apple with an arrow as part of his signature.*

Christ Methodist Church in 1956 in Chicago's south side was on the advancing colour line. The real estate sharks knew the whites' properties would diminish in value as the Blacks moved closer, because no other whites would buy, so it was dangerous to sell to Blacks. When a Black family did succeed in moving into a block, the remaining whites would panic and sell to a realtor at a fraction of the value. The realtor would then inflate the price to two or three times what he had paid, and sell to Blacks. Some whites knew enough to hang on to their homes until the block began to change and then sell directly to Blacks.

When whites lost money on their homes, they directed the blame to the Blacks, and not to the unscrupulous realtors where it belonged.

When we arrived at Christ Church, the first Black families had already moved into the block. The real improvement for us was the larger parsonage. Our salary increased from $3200 to $4200 per year. The congregation was creatively grappling with racial change. They felt that the church's mission was to serve whatever people lived in the neighbourhood regardless of race.

There were no Black members yet. One Sunday a few weeks before we got there Elizabeth Johnson sauntered into the Service, the first Black to do so. A few members walked out - but most remained, and some welcomed her after the service, inviting her to come back. She later told us she attended solely to shock the whites.

One morning in 1956 we received a phone call from San Francisco: "Your son is here - why aren't you here to meet him?" The travel information sent by Mrs. Sawada never reached us.

Noting the chronic depletion of joint bank account #3077-44, we borrowed plane fare again. Bonnie made a lunch and was off. She found our son in a San Francisco Social Centre where he had been put up for the night. The boy, age six, was all smiles and keen to go along with Bonnie to his new home. We named him William Tell Cappuccino.

William, second from left, in Japan

Machiko, now also age six, had known William in the orphanage and he apparently knew her as well. But Machi had forgotten all her Japanese and William didn't know any English. They communicated in sign language, along with a profusion of words in their own languages. We were not aware of any other trans-racial adoptions in Chicago, or anywhere in Illinois.

A good article came out in *Ebony* (March, 1957) about our three children and our experience in our first two churches. It helped to let the Blacks in the community know that our church seriously wanted to serve all people.

Later on at a family reunion in New Jersey, William climbed a tree, taking his cousin Kathi Gentile with him. He could get down, but Kathi couldn't. Someone had to bring a ladder to the rescue. On another occasion, Kathi, trying to shinny up the trunk of a tree after William, got stuck about 25 feet up. He was secure a few feet higher on a branch, so he reached down, grabbed her wrist, and held her hanging in mid-air until help came. [7]

When we first got to Christ Methodist Church, a local white child told us she had counted 13 Black families in the block, which was composed of about 20 duplexes on each side, a total of 80 apartments. During our four-year stay, the community gradually changed so that only a few whites remained in the block. The new Black homeowners were highly conscious of their property and extremely neat. People whom I didn't even know would chase children from our church lawn. Being the largest lawn in the block, and enclosed by a low hedge, it was an ideal place for rassling. One day a Black woman scolded some children, "How

[7] Kathi survived to become an obstetrician. William became a high school teacher.

are we going to keep any grass there if you children play on it? You have a big sidewalk to play on."

The first Blacks who moved in organized themselves into a Block Club. I attended and was invited to be chaplain. Not wanting to offend the existing holder of that office, I demurred. But he begged me to relieve him of a role he didn't feel comfortable with. I think he was a carpenter. He might well have been a better chaplain than I, but I finally agreed, to show solidarity.

As more Blacks moved in, the density became greater. The public school put up a new addition, and as soon as it was opened it was overcrowded. Since the Blacks couldn't move into white areas, two or three families had to team up to be able to afford the inflated prices for the homes they were allowed to buy.

Blacks were intimidated in several ways. One was with fire protection. A block from the church there was a Black family who attended our services. They had a small fire in their kitchen and called the fire department. The engine that arrived first was, unfortunately, a white unit. The firemen rushed into the house. One of them quickly doused the fire. The rest took their axes and smashed all the windows in the house "to let the smoke escape." They also made holes in the plaster. Chicago Blacks endured this type of abject hatred for generations.

When I went around to make a pastoral call, our first Black member, Elizabeth Johnson, seemed hostile initially, but she was intrigued by our adopted Black children. One day she told us about her feelings for whites. She had suffered terribly at the hands of whites. Now her favourite pastime was to answer the door when a white person was knocking, and to respond, with a wide grin, "No, thank you," and slam the door in their face. She would do this regardless of what the person had to say.

After getting to know Bonnie and me a little better, she made two exceptions to her conviction that all whites were evil. One evening at our home, she said, "I'm considering adopting a child, but of course it would have to be a Black child."

Bonnie looked her in the eye and said, "Elizabeth, you're talking through your hat. If something happened to Fred and me, you would gladly take three-year-old Robin Hood to your heart, and you would be a wonderful mother to him." Elizabeth's mouth dropped open - she was stunned and speechless. She rushed out of the house. The next day she admitted that, of course, she really could love even a white child. She became a strong supporter in the congregation, and later was elected President of our Women's Society.

Elizabeth told us our William was known in the neighbourhood as Sammy Davis Junior – he was so friendly and charismatic.

One time Robin fell against the living room door. He was bleeding above his eye, so Bonnie asked a neighbour to watch the other two kids while we rushed Robin to the hospital. The doctor said he needed three or four stitches. As the doctor started on Robin, I began to feel queasy, left the room before I would faint, and sat on a chair outside. Brave Bonnie stuck it out. A few minutes later the stitches were done and she hobbled out with Robin, sat in a chair, head back, and fainted dead away, sliding halfway to the floor before I could catch her.

In 1957, around the stockyards area of Chicago there were half a dozen Protestant ministers who met to commiserate and celebrate with each other. One fellow asked us if we would agree to an experiment in "group therapy" for his thesis. We decided that while we were all perfectly sane, we would condescend to be guinea pigs for the sake of our friend.

At our first session, we all bound ourselves to secrecy. Several of us confessed to some behaviour we regretted. After that first session, we decided we wouldn't get anywhere unless our wives were there with us, because, after all, *they* were the ones with the problems.

So we invited the wives, who were delighted at this chance for extra communication with the husbands. We hired two women to sit with the group's 14 children in a church hall on Thursday mornings while the 12 parents sat around a big table in another room and talked. There was perfect attendance for the six-month duration of the group.

One fellow admitted to an overweening dislike for old people, a surprising vocational handicap. This same fellow also felt that in these modern times we should experiment with such things as swapping partners. He introduced the subject seriously, and said, "In fact, I move it." His wife didn't say anything. The motion lost for lack of a second.

One husband and wife could not communicate with each other on a deep personal level except in this group. At the Thursday meetings they would level with each other, but alone with each other at home, they were aliens. As a matter of fact, there were two such couples in our small group.

Each of us learned a lot. What I learned turned my life around 180 degrees. I had started out with the noble attitude that I was doing the Lord's work. Any time I had left from doing the Lord's work would be devoted to family.

Gradually an *insight* pushed its way through my thick skull, and a light went on: Bonnie was *also* doing the Lord's work. If anything, she was more deeply committed than I was. So I came to the - one might say - absurd realization that my first duty is to my wife, and *together* we would do the Lord's work. [8] Little did I realize at the time what I was getting myself into.

We still fight and holler at each other, mainly because she is so very stubborn. (I'm not.) But no matter how severe our arguments, separation or divorce is never an option - never mentioned, even jokingly. British actress Sybil Thorndike was asked whether she ever considered divorce from her husband. She said, "Divorce - never. But murder often."

---

[8] We now use a different idiom, a loosely worded "commitment to humankind."

The car with no reverse bringing home a donated stuffed chair

We had what I called a forward-looking car. We often had a problem with our car: the reverse konked out. Try parking a car every day with no reverse. Thankfully, the reverse did work for a few seconds when the engine was cold so I could back up to get out of the parking space in front of our house.

One day, 45 minutes from home the engine gave out. There we stood, loaded up with kids, and a big stuffed chair that someone had given us tied down on top. I called one of my Methodist minister friends who lived out there. He graciously pushed us with his own car for several blocks. I was just ready to give up when the old engine kicked in and roared. Robin Hood's remark summarized the incident, "Our family is so lucky. We have so much friends."

Meanwhile, the Meyer family in Madison, Wisconsin, had just adopted a child whom they named Steve. Steve was looking through *Ebony* at a neighbour's house and recognized our William. He ran home with the magazine to show his mother and, spouting Japanese, pointed to William's pictures and in English said, "My brother, Kunio" (William's earlier name).

The Meyers couldn't understand what he was saying, but the article verified that indeed the boys came from the same orphanage. They wrote to us and a wonderful family friendship blossomed. Steve had actually come across the ocean with William.

William as a teenager

The Meyers had seven children, all adopted. One of them was Martha, a four-year-old girl who had one good arm, but the other arm was developed only a little past the elbow. She was born that way.

When I first saw little Martha, I felt so sorry for her because she had only one good arm. But Martha herself seemed to be very happy. She could brush her own long blond hair with one arm; she could dress herself with one arm; she could put on her socks with one arm; she could

45

eat her breakfast with one arm; she could ride a tricycle with one arm. Machiko asked Flora Meyer if Martha felt sad about having only one arm.

Flora Meyer said "Martha gets into enough trouble with one arm - I don't know what I would do if Martha had two arms. She would probably get into twice as much trouble."

In spite of the distance between us (a four-hour drive each way), our friendship developed into one of the best friendships two families ever had. We needed each other.

Chapter 5

Irregular Heart Beat – Our Second-Born

Pierre Ceresole Cappuccino *arrived in 1957. Pierre Ceresole, a Swiss pacifist, founded the International Volunteer Service movement. He was called "Dreamer with a Shovel". Volunteers from many countries worked together to rebuild communities after a catastrophe. He tried to prevent WWII by speaking with leaders of enemy countries and suffered imprisonment several times.*

The year was 1957. Bonnie was doing all the exercises necessary to deliver our second baby born to us without anaesthesia. Her obstetrician was Dr Bayley. All the pregnant ministers' wives used to go to him. His father was my colleague, a Methodist minister.

When Bonnie arrived at the hospital he noticed an irregular heartbeat. He assured her, "Everything is all right; I don't expect any problem, and we'll keep a close watch. Emergency equipment is ready across the hall to get the baby out in a hurry if we have to, but I don't think we'll need it." Then he said, "Yours is such an unusual case I'd like your permission to allow the student nurses to learn something from it. Could they come in and see you?" Bonnie agreed. One should be willing to promote scientific research.

In they came. Each one stood over Bonnie, smiled, said "Hi," and held the stethoscope to Bonnie's belly listening to the faint irregular heartbeat of the baby. When they were through, they'd say, "Thanks" or "Good Luck" and leave the stethoscope on her belly for the next person.

After eight or ten of these tete-a-bellies, it got to be too much for Bonnie. Doctor Bayley again gave her the option of an anaesthetic. She said yes.

It was a boy. The irregularity had been caused by the umbilical cord wrapped around his arm. Again, we had no boy's name picked out. If it had been a girl, she would have been Annie Laurie. We settled on Pierre Ceresole Cappuccino.

On returning home after four days in the hospital, Bonnie was amazed at the growth of three-year-old Robin. He had been a little baby before. Now, he was huge. Someone had told us to measure Robin's height on his second birthday. It was three feet, one inch. This figure is supposed to double when they are full grown. Robin finally stopped growing at six feet two.

Some of the ladies of Christ Church really took to little Pierre, at age three, with his fiery red hair. One day several of them were fawning over him and it became too much. He spouted, "Old Bossy Cow!" They all laughed and tried to evoke another response. But that was all they could get out of him. They loved him to bits and couldn't get enough of him.

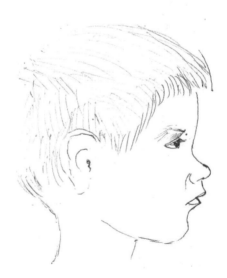

**Sketch of Pierre. Modesty prevents his father
from revealing the name of the artist**

Bonnie believes that *children tend to behave the way they are expected to behave*. When Pierre tended to be a little rough with the guinea pigs, she would say, "See how gentle Pierre is with the guinea pigs?" And gradually Pierre did become gentle when he picked them up. Another child-rearing principle was not to label a child: "This one tells lies" or "This one always spills her milk." Rather, we would say, "He's going through a stage – he'll be over it soon." That was usually the way it worked out.

Because of our interest in intentional community, we visited a Bruderhof centre in western Pennsylvania. The approximately 200 members lived in a former hotel four stories high in the Allegheny Mountains near a lake. Each family was allotted an apartment commensurate with the number of children.

When one joined the Bruderhof, all one's property was turned over to the community, in New Testament fashion. Their financial base was *Community Playthings* which made and sold large durable wooden toys - cars, trucks, trains – all made with industrial wheels, and axles of heavy steel, unbreakable.

There was a Baby House. A few members cared for all the infants so their parents could be freed to do daily assigned tasks. The parents would pick up their children after work. Nursing mothers came to their baby when needed.

We concluded that we really could not live with such a narrow theological perspective. But also, there was no way Bonnie would surrender the care of her babies to any other human being. That was her special joy.

We later heard that a rift developed in the community because all the "community property" was in fact registered under the Leader's name.

Chapter 6

Cute Kid from Korea

Annie Laurie Cappuccino *arrived in 1958. She was named for her two grandmothers, Anna Cappuccino and Laura McClung, and also for the song.*

As soon as Pierre was born Bonnie began agitating for another child. I said four was enough. She insisted that we needed another girl: "In the ideal family each child should have at least one brother and one sister." Machiko didn't have a sister.

Bonnie heard about an Oregon farm couple, Bertha and Harry Holt, who were bringing in orphan children from Korea. The Holts adopted eight all at once. They also set up an adoption agency. They were evangelical Christians and placed children only with families who were "saved." We didn't know if we qualified as "saved." Bonnie wrote to the Holts, telling them we would like to adopt a Korean orphan, and would be willing to accept a handicapped or a mixed-race child.

Regarding being "saved," each of us stated that we had an "experience of God" in junior high school. That seemed to satisfy the Holts and we received a picture of a forlorn looking little girl who had had polio, which impaired one leg. The picture showed an adorable child with curly hair. A picture is almost like a birth. The child becomes ours, and the long wait only adds to the feeling that she really is a part of our family.

Bonnie was already in Oregon when the chartered plane arrived from Korea with 120 orphans. As the children were brought in, the parents' names were announced and they came forward to receive their child. There wasn't time to be given any instructions about individual children. We knew they all might have head lice, which our child did - 77 of them (or was it 78?).

She had little pink knitted booties on her feet. Bonnie dressed her in the clothes we had been told to bring to Oregon. The clothes she came in went back to Korea. No suitcase - she came to us with no worldly goods whatsoever. At last we were able to use the name Annie Laurie

On the way home Bonnie had to hold Annie Laurie all the way. This was before airlines were fussy about seat belts. Not for an instant would the child allow Bonnie to put her down, which made for some inconvenience in times of personal urgency. It helped to have a bag full of small toys, pipe cleaners, books, etc. But what she wanted most was soda crackers. She had to have one in each hand. As she daintily consumed one she would fuss until that one was replenished, so she always had two.

Bonnie was also bringing back a small baby for another Illinois couple who, after they paid the plane fare for the child to cross the ocean, could not afford to go to Oregon to pick up the baby. So Bonnie brought theirs in a baby carrier provided by the airline.

Annie Laurie arrived on St Patrick's Day, 1958. She was 22 months old and weighed 22 pounds. On her first night at our home Bonnie sprayed her head with Raid, to get rid of the 77 lice (or maybe 78), a procedure recommended by the Holt Agency. Then Bonnie went around while all the rest of the family were sleeping and sprayed the rest of our heads as well - as a preventative. Soon after that we were all deathly sick. It might well have been the Raid that flattened us. But it did get rid of the lice.

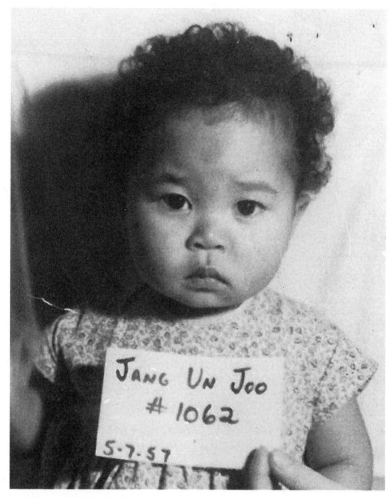

Annie Laurie in Korea. Jang Un Joo was her name back then

Dr Sam Banks, an orthopaedic surgeon, began a series of operations on Annie Laurie that would partially correct the damage done by polio. Polio was already rare in the U. S. and not all the doctors knew how to treat it, so Annie Laurie became Exhibit A. Dr Banks would show the student nurses and interns what he was doing with her. He never charged us for the numerous times he did surgery on her.

Meanwhile, we sang a lot of songs after meals. This one we sang almost daily:

Maxwelton's braes are bonnie
Where early fa's the dew,
And 'twas there that Annie Laurie
Ga' me her promise true...
Ga' me her promise true. Which ne'er forgot would be
And for bonnie Annie Laurie, I'd lay me doon and dee.

Her brow is like the snow-drift.
Her throat is like the swan.
Her face it is the fairest
That e'er the sun shone on...
That e'er the sun shone on, And dark blue is her e'e,
And for bonnie Annie Laurie, I'd lay me doon and dee.

Like dew on the gowan lying
Is the fa' o her fairy feet,
And like wind in summer sighing
Her voice is low and sweet.
Her voice is low and sweet, And she's a' the world to me
And for bonnie Annie Laurie, I'd lay me doon and dee.

It didn't take long before our new two-year-old recognized something special about this song. We'll never forget the day she realized the song had *HER NAME* in it. Her eyes grew larger. Then with a roar of laughter we all entered the exquisite joy of that moment.

The next day we were singing it again. When we came to the "Annie Laurie" part, she hollered out: "And Pierre, and William, and Machi, and Robin," all on the same note.

From early on Annie Laurie showed her independent spirit. We had not heard her use any English words, except "No." One day we were driving somewhere in the car, with most of the kids in the back seat – again, before seat belts - and Annie Laurie hollered something, probably in Korean. Bonnie inquired, "William, are you bothering Annie Laurie?"

"No, I'm not."

Immediately, Annie Laurie countered, "Yesadid! Yesadid!" - her first sentence in English. We all laughed, including William.

Another expression she used in a dialog with Pierre, a few months younger was "Sickantired! Sickantired!"

We had heard that Koreans are the Irish of the Orient. It's true.

Top, William, Robin, Machi. Bonnie is holding rambunctious Pierre. I'm holding Annie Laurie, at my folks' home in Scranton, Pennsylvania

Chapter 7

Baby Under the Coat - Our Sixth Child

Michael Scott Cappuccino *arrived in 1959. The Rev. Michael Scott was an Anglican clergyman from England who was unofficially speaking for the tribes of Southwest Africa at the United Nations. The US government confined him to a few blocks' radius because of his "radical" philosophy. His philosophy was freedom for all people. He also led a non-violent protest against French nuclear testing in Africa.*

In 1959 one of the 103 agencies to which Bonnie had written four years earlier wrote: "Our records show that you have one child and wish to adopt a second one - of mixed race." Mrs Isabel Sheffner, Director of Adoption Services in Aurora Illinois wanted a good home for a nine-month-old baby. His skin was very light, but now they were thinking he might have some Black genes mixed in. Apparently, as his hair grew it became tightly curled, and as the summer progressed he had become a little darker, and the adoptive family were not prepared for a Black child. It was September, and sounded like a suntan to Bonnie, but she didn't say anything. Mrs Sheffner asked us to give it some careful thought and let her know.

Bonnie and I thought about it. We sat down and considered all aspects and all the pros and cons. That took 13 minutes and 17 seconds. Bonnie called her back saying we'd dearly like to have him.

It became clear that, "For unto every one that hath (more) shall be given…" [9] Acquiring children is like acquiring money. If you have lots,

---

[9]   Matthew 25:29

it's easy to get more. Mrs Shefner had called a Unitarian minister friend, the Rev Charles Lyttle, who told her that his son, Brad Lyttle often came to our house for all-night envelope stuffing of various mailings for world peace. In his opinion we would be good parents.

At the foster home, there he was on the living room floor, vigorously working with his toys. He was ignoring people, and *doing* things. Now it was toys; later it would be hammers; then cars; then computers. We named him Michael Scott. We were staying with Bonnie's folks overnight. When we arrived our five other children were surprised when I opened my overcoat – and there he was.

Michael at the foster home before we picked him up

56

One day around the kitchen table we were discussing where everyone came from. William said, "I came from Japan"

Robin: "I was born from Mommy."

When we got to Annie Laurie, she said, "We adopted me."

Top, Machi, Robin, William. Bottom, Michael, Annie Laurie, Pierre

Annie Laurie had beautiful little cheeks. She also had her own way of thinking. Once she told Bonnie, "Mommy, I have a headache."

"Where?" Annie Laurie thought for a moment, and then placed her little forefinger on the middle of her cute cheek.

When Annie Laurie was three she became more articulate. One day she said to Bonnie, "Mommy, you have a big fanny. By Golly, you have a big fanny." (Not at all true – FC.)

She was also learning about door knobs. She went around opening and closing doors all over the house. One day when I was out, Bonnie was startled to find a complete stranger in the living room. How long he had been sitting there we didn't know. Annie Laurie had heard him rapping at the door and assumed that he wanted a sandwich, so she opened the door and invited him to "come in - sit down in there." She was so busy with other important matters that she neglected to mention his presence to Bonnie, who discovered him some time later and fed him.

Annie Laurie and the homeless man

During the 1959 steel strike an average of fifteen homeless men a week were coming to our door for a meal. The strikers were competing with the homeless for the lower paying casual jobs. A very few were alcoholics; many were despondent, having reached the bottom. One Irishman who said he never drank also said he couldn't find work. "Nobody wants to hire you when you're 59 years old." Some men never said a word from the time they introduced themselves with, "Can I get a bite to eat?" Bonnie usually had a big pot of food for these situations. Once several men came to the door, and all they said was, "Is this the place?" and later, "Thank you very much." When we asked, some said they walked from downtown Chicago. That was eight miles away through the snow.

Shortly before Christmas, Bonnie had just put some warm cupcakes into the breadbox. I thought I'd sample some. No sooner did I have the lid open when Bonnie slammed it down again: "Don't touch those! - they're a Christmas treat for the men! You can finish Saturday's cake." The wherewithal for all this largess came from joint bank account #3077-44. The longer I knew her, the more mystery she radiated.

Bonnie with Michael

Several times we visited Bonnie's aunts and uncles and her grandfather, Hugo Mueller, in Minnesota. Our six children were enthralled with their only great grandparent. In fact, Annie Laurie, age three, asked him to bend his head down so she could comb his hair. He did.

At Bonnie's mother's place in Illinois. Top, Robin, Laura Mueller McClung and Laura's father Hugo Mueller from Minnesota. Bottom left, Annie Laurie, William behind Machi, Pierre, Michael in Bonnie's lap

**Clockwise from left, Machiko, Annie Laurie,
Robin, William, Pierre, Michael**

Senator Joe McCarthy loomed large in our lives. He was elected to the
U.S. senate from Wisconsin in 1946 and gained power by pointing to what he
considered a threat – communism. In February 1950 he famously said, *"I have
here in my hand a list of 205…names…known to the Secretary of State as being members
of the Communist Party…"* He saw communists everywhere. A lot of ordinary
Americans were hoodwinked by his diatribes, resulting in mass paranoia.
Hundreds of Hollywood actors were black-listed and their careers ruined. My
own name was on several "lists". A Methodist colleague was jailed because he
would not reveal the names of people who attended his summer camp. There
was a climate of fear across the land which was only partially eased with his
death in 1957.

In Chicago in 1959 during the dark days following the death of Senator
Joe McCarthy, the word "peace" was still suspect as a communist word.

61

Some pacifist groups wanted to challenge this way of thinking and planned a Peace March down Michigan Avenue on the day before Easter. I went to a training session where I was instructed in Gandhian non-violence, and I was proud to receive a blue arm band signifying that I was one of two dozen marshals to keep a semblance of order, and to interpret the march to reporters.

That Saturday morning Bonnie was painting the kitchen yellow. At the last minute she said, "I'm coming to the peace march. It will be good for the children." At that time Bonnie had only two pairs of shoes. We were running late and she forgot to change from her old tennis shoes which were splotched with yellow paint. More often than not we had three babies in diapers. We loaded our six kids and the collapsible buggy into the car and headed off.

At Michigan avenue we uncollapsed the buggy and dropped in the babies - three-year-old Annie Laurie, two-year-old Pierre, and one-year-old Michael. I was wearing the blue arm band and had to go up and down the line. Bonnie had three in the buggy, and walking ahead of her were our three older kids: Robin Hood, five, and Machiko and William Tell, both nine. They were proud to be there.

During the march I was pre-occupied with the eight or nine hundred marchers. I was conversant in Gandhian philosophy and was all ready for reporters' questions. But I didn't see a reporter all day long. The dumb reporters were all talking to this dame with yellow paint on her shoes and too many kids in a dilapidated buggy.

Once when we were visiting Bonnie's folks, her brother David was home on furlough from the U. S. Marines. He always liked our kids, and he could see Bonnie had her hands full with three in diapers. He asked, "Is there anything I can do to help?"

"Well, if you really want to help, you can take these diapers to the Laundromat."

"Sure." and off he went with a huge bundle.

When he returned, Bonnie said, "What did you tell them at the Laundromat?"

"I told the lady to 'Wash'em, starch'em, and iron'em.'" He didn't understand why Bonnie broke out laughing. She immediately opened the package. The diapers were all fluffy - the lady fortunately hadn't followed U. S. Marine procedure. But David's heart was in the right place, and Bonnie really appreciated his help.

Even though the members at Christ Church (mostly Black) wanted us to stay, I felt it was time to move on. I knew the church wouldn't grow unless they could get a minister who had more rhythm in his preaching. My sermons had precious little "Soul."

Another factor was safety and security. One night at two in the morning the bed-side phone rang. A neighbour said in a low voice, "Someone's trying to get in your window." In the dark we looked and could see the silhouette of a youth outside slowly withdrawing. He had heard the phone. We had five other break-ins or attempted break-ins during our latter days in that parsonage.

Sometimes on their way to school other kids made William jump up and down so they could confiscate any loose change on him. Also, the public school became difficult. With the burgeoning population the new school addition was already overcrowded from the first day it opened. Children attended in shifts, from 8 a.m. to Noon, or Noon to 4 p.m. One of our children had a learning disability. We had to move. We had spent four eventful and pleasant years at Christ Church. Our congregation had changed from all white to virtually all Black without any racial incident. They retained the white janitor.

Chapter 8

Farming Country

In 1960 we told the District Superintendent we would accept another "difficult Charge." We moved to Winslow, Illinois, 135 miles west of Chicago where we acquired a circuit of three churches. Very few ministers wanted to travel a circuit on Sunday mornings. I loved it.

Three local families were opposed to an inter-racial family living in their town. None was in the congregation. One was the barber, who vowed that he would "never cut any nigger's hair." This was okay with us, since Bonnie was cutting our kids' hair as well as my own.

The second fellow worked at one of the gas stations. We stayed out of his way and bought our gas at the other station, but later he finally began to speak to us.

Third was the poorest family in town. With our arrival they finally had someone to look down upon. Shortly before we arrived, the husband on a dark night had stolen a cow, intending to butcher it. The only place he had to hide a cow was his garage. But he hadn't calculated on the MOOOO factor. It didn't take the owner long to find the noisy critter. No one pressed charges.

All our children were well integrated into the schools and into the community. When they misbehaved we heard about it just as any other parents did. One incident involved Robin in First Grade. His teacher was a loving, capable woman who was a member of the Evangelical United

Brethren Church, more conservative than ours. Six-year-old Robin began asking questions when he came home from school, such as, "Mommy, do we believe in heaven?"

Her answer was sometimes a little indirect, such as, "Well, some people believe there is a heaven up in the sky."

"But what do WE believe?"

Bonnie would tell him, little knowing that he was in the middle of an ongoing theological debate with his teacher in the First Grade classroom. The teacher had attempted to explain Easter to her class. She said, "Isn't that so, Robin?" assuming that the minister's son would corroborate her views.

Robin's thoughtful response was, "Well, my Daddy doesn't think it happened exactly THAT way."

"But Robin, it says so in the Bible."

"Well, my Daddy doesn't think EVERYTHING in the Bible is true - he thinks some of it is true, but some of it is like a fairy tale." The teacher was more than a little shocked. She honed her arguments more carefully. Everyone in town knew about this, but it was months before Bonnie and I heard of it.

Meanwhile, our smallest congregation, Basswood, learned that I didn't believe in Hell, and they thought, "If there were no Hell, then why would people be good?" Without fear of Hell the whole moral fabric of society would fall apart. The congregation had no confidence in anything I might say to them after that.

At Winslow a different problem arose. Michael, age three and Pierre, age four, were standing at the top of our front steps, having a contest to see who could urinate the farthest. As two liquid arcs were splattering the lowermost steps and sidewalk, one of the church trustees drove by. She was not amused at seeing this desecration of not only parsonage property (the steps), but also town property (the sidewalk). Unfortunately, from her complaint we could not ascertain which of our boys won the contest.

**Robin, on the way to Grade One, standing on the parsonage steps
where Pierre and Michael had an infamous contest**

Pierre came home from school one day, and announced with a great
sense of accomplishment, "I finally found out what 'F - U - C - K' spells."

Bonnie said, "Hmm," planning in her mind how she would go about
sex education for a six-year-old.

Then Pierre said, confidently, "It spells 'fart'."

In Winslow Bonnie heard about a town women's organization and
wanted to show she was a friendly person, so she inquired when the next
meeting was so she could attend. Her friend said, "They will have to vote
before a new member is accepted, so they will tell you after the meeting."
Bonnie was shocked. She decided never to be a member of an
organization that has to vote on new members.

In our Methodist Sunday School William happened to question some statement of the teacher. After a pause, her nervous response was, "Well, that's what it says in the Quarterly, so that's what we'll believe." Bonnie disliked this close-mindedness at Sunday School so much that she allowed our kids to stay home if they wished. Meanwhile, we applied to the Unitarians to see if we could transfer to them. Their Sunday schools are not doctrinal and are based more on child psychology.

Bonnie felt a little like Phyllis McGinley, an American poet and author, who wrote:

Ah, snug lie those that slumber
Beneath Conviction's roof.
Their floors are sturdy lumber,
Their windows weatherproof.

But I sleep cold forever
And cold sleep all my kind,
For I was born to shiver
In the draft from an open mind.

Michael, Pierre, Annie Laurie

Chapter 9

Maryland – Our Seventh Child

Mohanlal Ananda Cappuccino *arrived in 1964. He was born in the U.S. of Tamil and Singhalese parents from Sri Lanka, hence the Hindu first name and Buddhist middle name. Mohan is another name for the god Krishna, and is also the same root as Gandhi's first name. Lal means jewel. Ananda means peace of mind, and was the name of Buddha's beloved disciple.*

Having wooed the Unitarians for some time, I succeeded in getting certified. It was painful to leave the Methodists. (In Canada the Methodists merged with other denominations in 1925 to become The United Church of Canada.) For one thing, Methodists sing better than Unitarians who, in 2005, produced a brand new Hymnal in which less than a quarter of the hymns are in four-part harmony. I love the Unitarians, but have to acknowledge that Unitarians, with notable exceptions, sing in black and white. Methodists sing in colour. The Black Methodist church we served in Chicago earlier sang in magnificent technicolour.

A woman called us from Montgomery County, Maryland: "We have read the material which the Unitarian headquarters in Boston sent about you. Would you be interested in moving to Silver Spring?"

Trying to mask my elation at this first nibble from Unitarians, I replied, "We're interested, but we're concerned about our mixed-race family. Isn't Maryland a southern state?"

"The rest of Maryland is 'south,' but Montgomery County is 'north' in its social attitudes. If it works out for you to move here, 155 church members would help you get settled." On a Saturday in December 1962, I was met at the Washington airport. After meeting with various committees, I was called to be the minister of the Unitarian Universalist Church of Silver Spring, Maryland.

The congregation helped us find a house – the first we ever owned. Up until now we lived in church-owned parsonages. Just outside the kitchen door was a huge red oak tree, with a trunk two feet across. Most of the year we ate all our meals outside on the picnic table under the oak.

Our house in Takoma Park, Maryland, 1963, with massive red oak behind

Around this time (1963) our whole family – as well as virtually the entire Silver Spring Unitarian Universalist congregation - participated in Martin Luther King's *March On Washington*, when Dr King delivered his memorable "I have a Dream" oration that cheered the hearts of two hundred thousand marchers. Our older children remember the experience vividly. King's message was Christian. It was also Gandhian to the core.

**From left: Pierre, Machiko, Robin, William, with
Fred holding Michael and Annie Laurie**

Every week we picketed "whites only" housing construction projects. Picketers came from widely varied backgrounds. Georgina Dunn was a Presbyterian with an authentic Scottish accent to prove it. Wherever there was a gathering for open housing or open hiring, Georgina was there, proclaiming the cause of the Blacks who still suffered severe discrimination.

One Sunday she showed up at our church and said to me, "I cam to join yir chirch."

I said, "Georgina, you're Presbyterian. What about our theological differences?"

"Wayll, the Unitarian theology asn't werth tiu pins, but I noticed on the picket line the Unitarians are always there, so I'm castin' me lot wi' yiu." And join she did. She was a delight and an encouragement to us all.

Pearl Buck, the American Nobel laureate, in her book, *My Several Worlds*, told of visiting an orphanage somewhere in the U.S. She asked, "How many children do you ordinarily keep here?"

The worker said, "200."

Pearl Buck said, "Well, it must vary some - sometimes a few less, sometimes a few more?"

"Oh, No, it's always 200. We can't let a child be adopted out until another comes in. If the number goes below 200, our state allotment decreases." Appalled, Pearl Buck founded her own adoption agency, Welcome House, which places children in adoptive homes immediately.

Pearl Buck said there are three options for an orphaned child: adoption, foster care, and the orphanage. Her opinion was that adoption is the best; a well-run orphanage is second best; and foster care is the worst option (although we know many couples who are providing excellent loving foster care).

In the summer of 1963 our family went to the annual adoption picnic in New Jersey. Attending were people who wanted or who had adopted children of races other than their own. The picnic was held at the small farm of the Lerkes, who had adopted seven children in addition to two born to them. There were rabbits, dogs, chickens, goats - a child's paradise. Mr and Mrs Lerke seemed relaxed in the midst of 200 people wandering in and out of their house.

Among the photos displayed was one photo of a girl of Greek and Ecuadorian-Aboriginal background - a child of seven, in a foster home in Florida. When the picnic was over, we told the Lerkes we would return in a week. During that week Bonnie decided we wanted to adopt the little Ecuadorian-Greek child.

When we returned to the Lerkes we were startled to find this girl there, to be adopted by them. She had been living in a Caucasian foster home in Florida and had been discovered by some racial bigots. The agency moved her to another foster home, and she was again discovered. The third day, she was at another foster home, which was then bombed. She was rushed by the case worker to a hotel where they spent the night. The case worker then called up Welcome House in Pennsylvania and asked if they would have a home that very day. The social worker there, Mary Graves, called the Lerkes and asked them if they would like to adopt this child. Mrs Lerke said, "Well, yes, we would."

"That's good, because I've already told them you would, and the child is on the plane."

This family, with nine kids already, made room for one more on a few hours' notice. The child was sent by air freight because the Florida agency was afraid she would cause a rumpus on a passenger flight. She was on a cargo plane without adult escort except the crew. The Lerkes went to LaGuardia Airport to meet her. At the freight terminal the pilot took her off the plane and turned her over to her new parents without a word to them. The agency record stated that this child was the brightest in her class at school. It also stated that she had had lye thrown at her. She was seven years old.

At the picnic, social worker Mary Graves explained Pearl Buck's feeling that children should be placed in adoptive homes immediately, without any foster home in between. Mary once asked Pearl Buck whether it might not be useful to have a foster home "for emergencies only," such as illness of prospective adoptive parents.

Pearl Buck's response was, "Well, you have a nice apartment. Such a child could just stay with you until the adoptive parents can take him or her."

Mary laughed, "So far there have been no emergencies requiring me to keep a baby at my place."

At one meeting Mary Graves mentioned that an East Indian baby was going to be born some months later, at the end of February, and would be placed for adoption. Bonnie poked me with her elbow, whispering: "That's our baby." But I was firm. Six was enough.

Our seventh child, Mohan, was born on March 7, 1964. He arrived in our home six days later. He was brought by Mary Graves to our home in Takoma Park, Maryland. There were five years between him and Michael, the next youngest, so he never lacked attention.

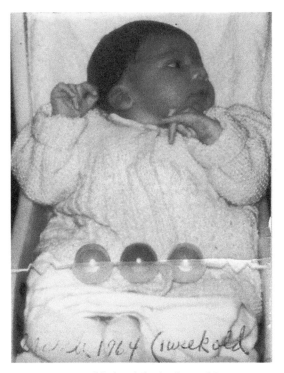

Mohanlal, six days old

Another adoptive parents' picnic was held at Pearl Buck's farm in Pennsylvania. Some 200 parents and children were there. Machiko especially enjoyed the picnic because she met a girl from the same orphanage in Japan who thought she remembered Machiko.

Machiko as a teenager

The one who enjoyed the picnic the most was Robin Hood, age ten. Being an avid reader, he knew something of Pearl Buck, so he pressed through all the people and found an opportunity to talk with her personally for a moment. "I read all your books." said Robin, which made her laugh. He had actually read all her children's books.

Bonnie asked, "What did Pearl Buck say to you?"

He said, "I don't remember. But *I talked with Pearl Buck.*"

We might mention here that Pearl Buck, who was raised by missionary parents in China, was devastating in her criticism of the missionary community: She told her audience that even as a girl she had chosen Kwan Yin, the Buddhist goddess of mercy, over the jealous angry God of the Bible. This was her advice to a novelist:

> *"Do not be born under the shadow of a great creed, nor under the burden of original sin, nor under the doom of salvation. Go out and be born among gypsies or thieves or among happy workaday people who live in the sun and do not think about their souls."* [10]

[10] p 178, Peter Conn, Pearl S Buck, *A Cultural Biography*, Cambridge University Press, 1996

Chapter 10

Selma Alabama

The movie, SELMA, which Bonnie and I found quite moving when we saw it in 2015, is a psychological study of Martin Luther King, Jr and his wife, Coretta Scott King, as well as President Lyndon Johnson. It's a good movie and worth seeing. But it missed the Gandhian dynamic, inspired by Dr King, of the five day non-violent stand-off between the marchers and the police, which, it seems to me, was the real significance of Selma, Alabama 50 years ago. Dr King, subpoenaed by the authorities was unfortunately not able to be present for this five day stand-off.

Bonnie's comment as we left the theatre was that James Reeb's character was miscast. He was not the wimpy stereotypical protestant minister. Jim actually stood tall and faced the world with courage.

In Selma, Alabama, a march by African-Americans demanding the right to vote was held. The march by 500 protesters crossed the Edmund Pettus Bridge on the way from Selma to the capital Montgomery. The police were waiting on the bridge, and on March 7, 1965, known as "Bloody Sunday", they beat back the marchers with nightsticks and tear gas.

National television was there, and the nation was shocked at the brutality of the police. Martin Luther King called upon all Unitarian and other clergy to come to Selma to support the marchers. The Rev James Reeb was among those who responded to the call. Jim was one of our Washington area Unitarian ministers, and had been on retreats together with us. When he entered a room, everything brightened up. He had a trace of mischief and a deep sense of humour that endeared him to us all.

On March 9th, 1965, as he was leaving a Selma restaurant with two other Unitarian ministers, a few angry whites followed them and from behind they hit Jim on the side of the head with a club. He fell, his skull smashed in by the blow.

When Ken Marshall and I heard that Jim had been badly wounded, we talked with our wives about going to the march. Bonnie, though apprehensive, agreed with my going. She felt it was important for our children to see we were taking a stand to ensure that all people, of whatever background, would be treated equally. Ken and I went together. In Selma, police cars encircled the nine-square-block Negro enclave. Some 260 Unitarian ministers were among the thousands of demonstrators in Selma.

After Bloody Sunday, Selma Police Chief Wilson Baker resigned in protest against the carnage. But because he was widely respected for his integrity and his common decency, the city fathers pleaded with him to stay on and take sole charge of dealing with the demonstrators. He accepted, I would imagine, with great trepidation. He was a segregationist and would not allow the demonstrators to march, but he had little patience with lawless hooligans.

Our goal was to march to the Court House and have a prayer service for Jim Reeb, and later, after he died, to have a memorial service for him. We lined up five abreast in front of the Baptist Church and walked forward to the line of police and ask to be allowed to pass through. Chief Baker refused. So we waited through the day, with a thin line of police straddling the road, facing hundreds of marchers standing 20 feet away. In the middle ground there was a civil rights leader on a soap box addressing the demonstrators, joking, and leading songs. Both groups stood there through the night, at times changing personnel so some could sleep and others maintain the vigil. This non-violent confrontation lasted for five days and nights.

Those who felt that they might be provoked into reacting with violence were asked to stay in the church and pray for their opponents. They all converted to pacifism!

The police were standing in a line for long hours. At one point Chief Baker got out of his police car and tied one end of a clothesline to a telephone pole. He walked across to the road and tied the other end to a tree. The rope was to take the place of his tired policemen. The marchers immediately composed a song:

We have a rope that's the Berlin Wall,
The Berlin Wall, the Berlin Wall,
We have a rope that's the Berlin Wall, in Selma, Alabama.

In an instant, someone composed a second stanza:
Hate is the thing that built this wall,
Built this wall, built this wall,
Hate is the thing that built this wall, in Selma, Alabama.

Then:
Love is the thing gonna make it fall,
Make it fall, make it fall,
Love is the thing gonna make it fall, in Selma, Alabama.

More stanzas were composed on the spot.

Earlier, during the orientation for newly-arrived ministers, an associate of Dr King, the Rev P T Vivian, explained that if they arrest all of us, we will willingly go. But if they try to take one, then we will lock arms, and they'll have to drag as many as are locked together. In jail we would be served "chopped greens," another term for grass.

"There is a certain dignity," said Vivian, "in walking to the paddy wagon and transforming it from what it is into a haven of freedom." At one point Chief Baker actually did place Vivian and Ken Marshall under arrest, and the whole group quickly locked arms. Baker had to laugh, and said, "Well, all right." He didn't arrest them when he saw what was happening.

On the second night it rained. A Black leader on the soap box said about Chief Baker: "He thinks it's great, this rain, and he think we'll go inside. He don't understand us. I need a bath anyhow." (laughter). Someone provided a huge sheet of plastic that would cover the width of the roadway and perhaps fifty feet back. We unrolled it and put umbrellas through the corners, and we were set for the night. After a while Chief Baker on the bullhorn told us, "You'll have to roll back the plastic. You're breaking the law."

"What law are we breaking?"

"There is a City ordinance saying there shall be no structure built without a permit." Everyone laughed. The ministers rolled the plastic back and stood in the rain, but the kids [11] behind them didn't want to get wet, so they kept part of the plastic cover. Baker let it go at that. He knew that if he did come and take the plastic, even that would have given us publicity points.

Another associate of Dr King was the Rev James Bevel. Some well-meaning politicians had been asking President Johnson to send down federal troops. Bevel said, "It is not federal troops that are needed in the South, and if that is our main purpose, we will fail." He felt that it was good for the ministers to come and he related the Selma experience to what was happening in Vietnam, for Bevel believed strongly in the power of non-violence. He said, "In our country we have a pattern of trying to solve everything by violence, but in reality, it solves nothing." He said, "I read in the paper and saw on TV that a few defenceless people in a plastic tent in Selma had more power than all of the military we sent to Vietnam. We need a non-violent approach of suffering to solve problems, not killing to solve problems."

On Thursday, when the death of Jim Reeb was announced, being Jim's friend, I was asked to offer the prayer. I don't usually pray, but it

[11] Young people in their teens and twenties were referred to as kids.

was a distinct honour to be on the soap box and pray at that time. Those days in Selma were a religious experience. I'm not easily moved to tears, but down there, many times something would occur and I would break down and cry, not for danger to myself but by a recognition of overflowing human nobility - sensing the courage of the people who lived in Selma. After all, we brave fellows who came down from somewhere else would return to our secure homes; these people would have to face the bigots.

An amusing aspect at Selma was that virtually every action taken by the police unwittingly helped the cause of civil rights. For example, at 2 a.m. Sunday morning our line was thinning out. People were tiring and disappearing into the homes. There was a little fire in a barrel in the road behind our line. Sheriff Clark decided to deprive us of this luxury, so all the fire engines in Selma came with blaring sirens to put the fire out. The people came pouring out of their houses, solving our problem of the thinning line for the rest of the night.

Apparently the police couldn't see that their cause was hampered by the "Berlin Wall". As long as people could not exercise their constitutional rights, the press reported it continuously. After a day and night of listening to the Berlin Wall song, Commissioner Baker got so tired of it that he suddenly got out of his car, deliberately walked over, took out his little pen knife and cut the rope.

The press gathered all around. Baker, just as abruptly, went back to his car and announced on his bullhorn, "I am confident that you will not march illegally, even if I have removed the rope - and, by the way, I would please like to have my clothesline back."

Just then, press photographers were taking pictures of kids cutting lengths of clothesline. Each kid had a three-inch piece of the Berlin Wall. Chief Baker made an involuntary contribution to the memorabilia of Selma.

The shoes I wore in Selma were old. One sole loosened from the front, and peeled off all the way back to the heel. With each step I had to kick my foot up to flip the sole back under, much to the amusement of my colleagues. Finally I got a short length of coat hanger wire, and hooked it around the sole and onto my shoelaces. That's how I saved my sole in Selma.

The miracle of Selma was loving your opponent, which was deeply ingrained into the hearts of the demonstrators by the speeches, by the songs. We sang:

We love Gov'nor Wallace, We love Gov'nor Wallace, We love Gov'nor Wallace, in our hea-rts - We love Gov'nor Wallace, We love Gov'nor Wallace, We love Gov'nor Wallace, in our hearts.
We love Chi-ief Baker..............
We love Sheriff Clark...............

Gradually we could sense some change of heart on the part of the authorities. In this face-to-face confrontation of kids and police officers, the kids tried to make the cops laugh. They'd do various funny things and, sure enough, some of the cops' shoulders would start to shake as they tried to suppress a laugh. One Black minister with a great voice was in front of the line. Between songs he would preach: "We believe in non-violence. That means we love our opponent. We love these policemen, don't we? Say Amen!"

The crowd thundered, "***AMEN!***"

He said, "These policemen in front of us have night sticks and they have guns in their holsters. The guns are loaded, but they don't want to shoot these guns at us," and he turned around to the police and said, "You don't want to use those guns on us, do you? Say Amen!"

And before they could think, several of the police hollered, "Amen!"

One person profoundly moved was Chief Baker himself. By day, he was a segregationist. But the world didn't know that at night, under cover of darkness, Baker would come into the Black church, and sit down with the leaders of the march. At one point he told them, "I don't want any more killings," and he broke down and wept. He said, "Please don't let [Sheriff] Jim Clark know I'm crying."

Baker was a segregationist, but in his heart he was a man of peace. He had had some training as a lawyer and also as a minister. He could spar intelligently with the ministers. On Sunday morning when the group wanted to have a prayer service at City Hall, Baker said, "You're not having a demonstration on Sunday morning in Selma, Alabama!"

A minister said, "We just want to pray."

Baker looked him in the eye and said, "If you want to pray, why don't you do the way God says, and go home and pray in your closet?" [12] Chalk up one up for Baker.

Someone asked, "May the Episcopalians attend the Episcopal Church?"

He had to ponder that for a while. Finally he said, "The Episcopalians may attend the Episcopal Church." The Episcopalians hurried through the police line. A multitude of Unitarian ministers, including Farley Wheelwright, converted to Episcopalianism that day and went along.

The Vestry of the Episcopal Church met them at the door. They said any minister could come in, Black or white, but the group couldn't come in as a whole. So they all stayed outside. A week later, *Life* magazine's cover showed our Unitarian colleague, Farley Wheelwright, devoutly kneeling and presumably praying on the church steps as an Episcopalian.

The march was totally non-violent. Finally, on March 15th, 1965, President Lyndon Johnson, a segregationist from Texas, on radio and television gave his memorable "We Shall Overcome" speech. He repeated that phrase several times. He said, "I am sending this day to the Congress a Voting Rights Bill" to make it a federal crime to interfere with anyone's right to vote. Each time he said "We Shall Overcome," there was a cheer from the demonstrators, most of whom had tears streaming down their cheeks.

Johnson was a master at getting legislation through Congress. It didn't take him long to get the bill passed. He did this knowing that the

---

[12] Matthew 6:6

Democrats would lose the Southland for many years to come. There is still much to do, but the Voting Rights Bill changed the political face of the United States.

While I was in Selma there was a demonstration at the White House. Bonnie and our kids, as well as many other Unitarians were there. When I got home and reported to the congregation, the church was packed. We sang many Selma songs, including:

O-oh Freedom, O-oh Freedom, O-oh Freedom - over me!
And before I'll be a slave, I'll be buried in my grave,
And go home to my Lord, and be free!

Chapter 11

Move to Pointe Claire, Quebec – Our Eighth Child

Tran Thai Tong Cappuccino *arrived in 1968. Tran Thai Tong was an 11th century king in Vietnam who gave up his kingdom to become a Buddhist monk, and by his example brought peace to the land.*

After four years it was time to leave the Silver Spring Church for several reasons. One issue was our early opposition to the Vietnam War, although most members became anti-war as time passed.

We heard from Lakeshore Unitarian Church in Pointe Claire, Quebec. At 280 members, it was larger than the Silver Spring congregation. [13] It was on the same island as exotic Montreal. A huge plus was that our five sons wouldn't have to worry about being drafted into the army. We disagreed with the propensity of the U.S. to sacrifice its youth in trying to police the world.

The Pulpit Committee presented me as their Official Candidate. In November, 1966, Bonnie and I went to Pointe Claire with two-year-old Mohanlal, who immediately became everyone's darling. I preached in Pointe Claire at 9:30 and 11:00. The congregation decided our fate at 8 p.m., while we were airborne for Maryland. When we got home someone phoned to tell us the vote was 96%. We would move February first, 1967.

This was our last Christmas in Silver Spring. The Silver Spring Church sanctuary was all glass. All around the inside there was a window ledge two and a half feet from the floor. Before the people arrived for the Christmas Eve (1966) Service, a woman was humming and going around the sanctuary

---

[13] The Silver Spring church grew from 155 members to 240 in four years.

lighting a candle on each window ledge. She got three-quarters of the way around before she noticed that all her candles mysteriously had gone out.

As she had been lighting them, two-year-old Mohan was following discretely, about three candles behind her, in the darkened sanctuary, doing what you're supposed to do with candles - blowing them out.

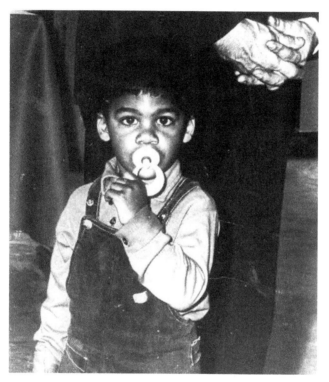

Mohan

Meanwhile, our realtor in Canada found Miss Agnes Houston and her six-bedroom house two blocks from the church. She was 84 and was pleased at the prospect of turning her house over to a minister with seven children. She said, "Children will make the house happy." When the realtor asked her about price, she said, "How much do you think the minister can afford to pay? Can he afford $10,000?" It was assessed at $24,000. The front room was 39 feet long, with a fireplace. When I phoned Bonnie, the feature most interesting to her was the six bedrooms. I'm sure she was thinking that with all that room we'd have space for more children, but she didn't say anything.

I was tempted to accept Miss Houston's offer of $10,000, but Bonnie wouldn't agree. We offered Miss Houston $18,000, the equity we got from our Silver Spring home. But Bonnie still felt we were taking advantage of her, so we asked her to talk it over with some trusted friends before she made a final decision. After doing this, she accepted our offer.

On February first, 1967, we arrived at the Canadian border. Only five of our seven kids were coming with us. William and Machiko stayed with family friends to finish High School in the States. After graduating they both decided to remain in the U.S.

**Top, Robin Hood, Mohanlal, Machiko, William Tell.
Bottom, Pierre, Annie Laurie, Michael**

**Same kids much later: top, Mohan, Pierre, Michael, Robin.
Bottom, William, Annie Laurie, Machiko**

Bonnie and I and our five kids became Landed Immigrants of Canada. February first was bitterly cold. Miss Houston's house was not ready yet. Half of our goods went with us to a rented town-house, the remainder to a friend's basement.

In May, 1967 we moved into 10 Bowling Green, Pointe Claire, where each of our five kids had a bedroom. The street was an upside-down U coming in from Lakeshore Drive, with a green park in the centre. The river could be seen from the house, with ocean freighters in the distance.

Mention was made earlier that one of our kids didn't like his name. But in Canada the Prime Minister was the charismatic Pierre Elliot Trudeau so our Pierre decided that his name was okay after all.

Our six-bedroom house on Bowling Green, Pointe Claire, Quebec

In 1968 British philosopher Bertrand Russell condemned the American slaughter in Vietnam as "genocide." Bonnie said to me, "If they're committing genocide, we can try to rescue at least one orphaned baby from over there."

I said, "We have enough babies. Besides, Canada is stricter than the United States. I've been told it's impossible to bring in overseas children to Canada for adoption.

"Then you don't mind if I try."

"Okay with me. Lots of luck."

Bonnie, Annie Laurie, Mohan, Fred, Pierre, Michael, Robin. Bonnie made the dress she is wearing

It didn't take her long to find out that another family had already succeeded. Lizette Gervais, a Quebec television personality, and her husband, Judge Robert Sauve, had adopted a Vietnamese child by proxy. Lizette's was the first adoption by proxy of an overseas child by a Canadian family. Her case was not hindered by the fact that her uncle was Jean Marchand, Minister of Immigration at the time. But she said to Bonnie, "I had to go through all the proper procedures. There's no reason why you can't do the same." With Lizette's step-by-step encouragement Bonnie asked for and received a Home Study from the Montreal Children's Service Centre.

Lizette had dealt with Rosemary Taylor, an Australian nurse with *Terre des Hommes* in Vietnam. Rosemary was rescuing G.I. babies, black and white, to be sent to the U.S. and Europe for adoption. Bonnie wrote letters to Lizette Sauve, to Rosemary Taylor, to Canadian government officials, and to Canadian adoption agencies. Finally we received a picture of a baby from Rosemary - a beautiful boy just a few months old. But because of Canadian red tape we couldn't get Canadian immigration papers for the child. We tried for months, until Rosemary informed us that the baby had died. We were devastated and became more resolute.

Our first baby in Vietnam – the one who died

Rosemary sent us a picture of another baby. We completed the adoption procedures in Vietnam, but we ran into more stonewalling at the Canadian Regional Immigration office in Hong Kong. One day when

Bonnie was particularly despondent, little Mohan said to her, "It's a lot easier to have a baby inside you. He would get here sooner."

Bonnie said, "Well, that takes a long time, too."

"But at least you know where he is," said four-year-old Mohan.

The first medical approval on this second baby was not sufficient for Canadian officials. They wanted to test him for syphilis by taking a specimen of spinal fluid! Rosemary Taylor refused absolutely. In war-time Saigon, with the lack of sanitation, any invasive procedure in an infant would have meant certain death.

Bonnie was horrified. This was *her baby* they were messing around with. She said, "Fred, you'd better get through to Pierre Trudeau, because this baby is also going to die if they keep playing around." I isolated myself in my study for two days to compose myself and to compose a four-page letter.

The Honourable Pierre E. Trudeau
Prime Minister
Ottawa

My Dear Mr. Trudeau:

We ask your help in obtaining an entry visa for our adopted infant son (6 mos. old) from Vietnam. Also, though we are not critical, we suggest that some fundamental changes in immigration procedures would be in order, to facilitate the entry of other adopted children into Canada.

The visa for our son was applied for in August '68 from the Canadian Immigration office in Hong Kong on our behalf by Miss R. J. Taylor, representative of Terre Des Hommes (the Swiss organization) in Vietnam. Our son has had all his exit papers for over a month and is ready to travel as soon as the entry visa is granted. His file number in Hong Kong is S.I. 1-106.

The cause of the delay seems to be the medical report. The first medical report was sent to Hong Kong in August, having been done by the Australian medical team in Vietnam. BECAUSE THE BABY WAS SO YOUNG, THERE WASN'T MUCH TO SAY OTHER THAN THAT HE WAS HEALTHY. This wasn't satisfactory to Hong Kong medical authorities, so they wrote the doctor in Saigon asking for more information, but by this time he had gone back to Australia.

By the time Miss Taylor learned of Hong Kong's desire for more information it was the middle of October. She immediately wrote asking Hong Kong what additional medical information was needed, and subsequently wrote several more times to Hong Kong, and never received an answer!

On Nov. 19 we called Hong Kong and spoke to Mr. Wales, superintendent of Canadian Immigration there, who told us that as soon as a new medical report came they would issue the entry visa. I asked him if Miss Taylor knew what was needed. He said, "Yes, we sent her a detailed list."

She never received this. I cabled that same evening to Miss Taylor to send a medical report. She immediately (Nov 19) sent off a medical report done by Dr. Barclay, a paediatrician on the British Medical Team at the Children's Hospital in Saigon.

I just received a letter from Mr. Wales (dated Dec. 3) which indicates that they have not received any letters from Miss Taylor since the first medical was received in October (although it had been sent in August).

Miss Taylor has been writing to me and complaining that her letters have not been answered by Hong Kong. THIS CONDITION OF THE MAILS MEANS THAT THIS NEW MEDICAL REPORT WILL PROBABLY NOT BE RECEIVED BY HONG KONG EITHER. Mr. Wales' letter to us was posted Dec. 3, two weeks after Miss Taylor's new medical report was mailed to him.

All this time OUR BABY IS CAUGHT IN THE MIDDLE because of the mail situation and the insistence of Hong Kong that they must have a "complete medical." Nothing wrong was indicated on the first report.

We have adopted five other children while living in the United States and we realize that adoption is - as is all the rest of life - a risk. Our youngest son, who is now four years of age, was placed in our home by Welcome House, Pearl Buck's Adoption Agency, when he was SIX DAYS OLD.

The only thing we could be sure of was that he was healthy - the same as we know by the first medical report on our baby in Vietnam. But because of the conditions in Vietnam we wonder how much longer he will remain in good health.

The first baby in Vietnam we had chosen died of pneumonia after he had been ill for only a few days, before we could get him to safety. We worry that this baby may get an infection and die also. Many babies are dying each day in all the orphanages.

It scarcely seems humane to insist on following the routine procedure under these conditions. We have tried to go through the regular channels, but this obviously is not accomplishing anything, and in the meantime our son is being deprived of the love and care he would receive in our family. This deprivation can have a stunting effect on his mental, emotional, and physical development, so instead of protecting us by insisting on a "complete" medical, we are being harmed.

We therefore ask you to send a request for the visa to be issued at once on the strength of a medical which showed him to be healthy. He could also be examined by the Immigration authorities at Dorval Airport when he arrives in Canada.

We also suggest in future cases of Canadian couples adopting Vietnamese children that because the mail between Saigon and Hong Kong is so unreliable some alternative system be set up. Perhaps the Montreal office can handle this. Miss Taylor has good communication with us because she uses an APO (American Army) address belonging to some friends. (She is Australian).

Miss Taylor is not paid for her work in helping adoptive couples, but volunteers her time and energy because she feels the need so keenly to get the children into families. She is very upset by the delay and all her efforts to no avail in this case, being already much overworked.

We are afraid she may refuse to help Canadian couples adopt unless some better system can be devised for obtaining entry visas for adopted Vietnamese children.

We were pleased by your warm offer earlier in regard to the Biafran children, and your intention of softening the regulations because of a state of emergency. This situation in Vietnam is also an emergency, and we hope you can see your way clear to aiding us for the sake of our infant son.

Very sincerely yours,

Fred Cappuccino, Minister
10 Bowling Green
Pointe Claire, QC

93

We mailed the letter to Prime Minister Trudeau on December 9, 1968. Bonnie, deeply frustrated with official callousness, announced to me: "I'm not going to eat anything until those guys in Ottawa open the door for my baby." Bonnie embarked on a Gandhian hunger fast. Trudeau's office would likely receive the letter on the 10th. On that day she didn't eat any breakfast or lunch. She and I were the only ones who knew about her fast. But if we didn't hear anything on the following day, I was going to call the newspapers, show them a copy of our letter to Trudeau, and tell them Bonnie was fasting until Immigration agreed to let the child in. Bonnie missed supper. At 7:21 p.m. that evening we got a phone call with a telegraphed message:

RE: YOUR LETTER TO THE PRIME MINISTER DATED DECEMBER 9 AND RECEIVED TODAY, IT IS RECEIVING IMMEDIATE ATTENTION. COPY OF IT IS BEING REFERRED BY HAND TO THE MINISTER OF MANPOWER AND IMMIGRATION [14] FOR URGENT ATTENTION. I AM SURE THE MINISTER WILL HELP YOU IN ANY WAY POSSIBLE. - WILLIAM G MORRIS, SECRETARY.

Bonnie ended her fast. All she could think of was her baby. She quietly ate a bowl of salad, breaking her fast at 7:55 p.m. the first day. A part of me was disappointed. What if the calloused bureaucrats had to deal with the publicity of a woman on a Gandhian fast? But all Bonnie wanted was her baby. Sometimes she doesn't have her husband's superior vision to see the larger picture.

On December 13 (Friday) at 5:12 p.m. 1968, a second telegram was phoned to us at home:

MR MACEACHEN HAS ASKED ME TO INFORM YOU THAT ALTHOUGH YOUR SON'S MEDICAL IS STILL

[14] The Honourable Allan MacEachen

INCOMPLETE, A VISA FOR HIM HAS BEEN AUTHORIZED
TO ENABLE HIM TO COME TO CANADA IMMEDIATELY.
TRANSPORTATION IS ARRANGED. MEDICAL TO BE
COMPLETED ON ARRIVAL AND IF IT IS SATISFACTORY,
CHILD WILL BE ADMITTED TO CANADA FOR
PERMANENT RESIDENCE.

- PETER C CONNOLLY, EXECUTIVE ASSISTANT TO MINISTER OF
MANPOWER AND IMMIGRATION, OTTAWA, ONTARIO.

This was a great relief to us, even though the promised "arranged" transportation never materialized. The baby would be on the first available plane. We named him Tran Thai Tong Cappuccino.

There had been no milk in the orphanage. He had been raised exclusively on rice water - the water the rice is cooked in. He was arriving in New York, so Bonnie flew down. My sister, Alice Gentile, and her daughter Betsy met Bonnie at the airport. They scurried over to another airport to meet the plane from Vietnam. The escorts had balloons tied to Tran for him to play with.

Back at Alice's, Tran slept in Betsy's dresser drawer, near Bonnie's bed. The next day Bonnie flew with him to Montreal. The immigration doctor didn't even examine him. He looked at the papers, looked at Tran, and said, "He's fine." This doctor was as horrified as we were that Canadian officials in Asia wanted to invade his spinal column. The rest of our family were all at the Montreal airport to meet this precious new arrival - always a joyful, joyful event.

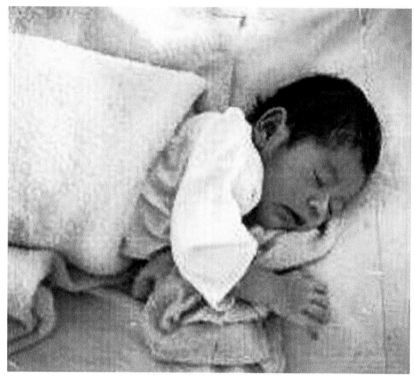

Baby Tran in Vietnam

Into our home this six-month-old brought head parasites, skin parasites, and intestinal parasites. But he was healthy, and at long last, we had him safely with us. Cappuccino Comments in *Lakeshore Unitarian Newsletter*, January 3, 1969:

Tran Thai Tong

How's that for a name to peal out the Old and ring in the New Year? Tran Thai Tong Cappuccino celebrated New Year's Day by flying from Saigon to New York, arriving in the wee hours of January 2nd. Bonnie flew down to meet him, and brought him to his new family the same day... Our paediatrician, who said Tran is four or five pounds underweight for a seven-month-old, also thinks Tran has a slight case of rickets...

Finally a letter to Trudeau's office wrought a miracle. "With man it was impossible, but with Trudeau all things are possible." (refer to Matthew 19:26)

Tran didn't smile for several days but he turned out to be a strong baby. The ones that survive are strong. When he cried, he really cried hard, sometimes holding his breath. Our doctor said there was nothing wrong - and presciently observed that maybe he just had a bad temper. Once again our family life was turned topsy turvy, adjusting to this new baby.

The Lakeshore News and Chronicle had a story and picture of Tran and Bonnie. That's when Sandra Simpson entered our lives. She lived around the corner and her kids played with our kids. One day she called Bonnie: "Please help me to get a baby just like yours." A few other couples came forward and we formed an informal adoption group, meeting at Lakeshore Unitarian Church. Families who had adopted interracially or who were hoping to do so gathered and shared ideas together with psychologists, social workers, and Black community leaders. Attendance often exceeded 60 persons.

We offered a prize of a bottle of wine to the member who thought up the best name for the group. Jody Boyer's entry, *"Families for Children,"* won her the bottle of wine.

At the meeting, wanting to get moving, I said, "Let's have nominations for President." Bonnie stopped me cold, saying, "Fred, you're going too fast." Then it hit me that this was not a routine task in the church which she routinely refused because she was too busy. This was something in which she wanted to play a major role. We slowly moved into an election mode. When we held elections Bonnie was elected president, Sandra was elected Vice-President and I became the Treasurer. In the beginning *Families for Children* was registered as a charitable non-profit organization. Later it became an adoption agency registered in Canada under the same name.

When Rosemary Taylor came from Vietnam and saw Tran, she couldn't believe how strong and healthy he was compared to other infants she had brought to Canada: "He's built like a Mack Truck," she said. He was about two years old.

Rosemary was fearless in Vietnam where war was waging. We looked upon her with a mixture of awe and anxiety. Everything depended on her. Sandra wanted a baby, and who knows how many more Bonnie wanted. Rosemary had her own style. A particular Vietnamese official's signature was required to legalize adoptions. After waiting in his office for days, Rosemary showed up in an outlandish dress and a big floppy hat. While he was laughing at her, she put the paper in front of him and said, "Please sign." He signed and Sandra got her baby.

Naomi and Herb Bronstein also applied for a baby. Naomi, impatient and persistent, bombarded Rosemary in Saigon with urgent telegrams. All she could think of was the baby she dearly wanted. Poor Rosemary was doing all she could, and felt Naomi was pushy. One time when Rosemary was bringing a convoy of babies to Montreal airport, Naomi heard about it and even though none of the children was for her, she showed up. As soon as Rosemary came through Customs, Naomi rushed up to her and said, "Hi. I'm Naomi Bronstein."

Rosemary took a full step back on meeting, for the first time, this woman who had been bombarding her for so long, but later on Naomi won Rosemary over and they worked together. Naomi, with deep compassion and a rollicking sense of humour, actually was a wonderful person to work with.

Our home was a temporary haven for several Vietnam War resisters. George Curiel crossed the border just before the U.S. authorities could nab him, and lived with us. Later we met his mother, Betty Rotundi, a New York trade unionist. She was a staunch agitator against militarism, and for peaceful revolution, although she had her own concept of "peaceful". After suffering permanent internal damage from a police fire hose she decided to wear spike heels to defend herself against brutal policemen. When she came to visit us, she was so enthralled with our children that she phoned her friend in New York: "You should see this wonderful family I'm visiting up here in Canada! They have a dozen children that they've adopted from all over the world and they're all named after revolutionaries!"

Betty took our kids fishing on the river bank. We had mixed feelings about her influence on them. She was an idealist who wanted a better world, but sometimes her methods were suspect. She absolutely despised "corporations". She told Robin to steal only from corporations and not people. She also told him that he shouldn't shop-lift because he was a long-haired teenager and everybody was watching him. But as a rather ordinary-looking middle-aged woman she was not watched at all and was able to "disappear" things quite easily. Anything she could do to hurt corporations was okay. Robin told us about it, and we were more watchful from then on. But we all loved her, and had long and noisy discussions about "fighting the corporate takeover." Now deceased, her personal life was sad. She said the main reason she came up to see us so often was that among all her friends we were the only couple still together.

Her son, George, meanwhile, started dating Shelly Bloomer, one of the bright young women of our congregation. Their wedding was in the front room of our house with all our children in attendance. The bride and groom wanted love beads. George brought two friends up from New York just to hold the beads - one a Black Power leader, the other a gay poet (Caucasian). At the service one held the beads to be placed on the bride, and the other held beads for the groom. After the couple exchanged rings, these words were spoken:

"As the rings symbolize the endless circle of love for each other, so the beads today symbolize the endless circle of love for humankind. (Beads were placed around the necks of bride and groom). Please accept the beads until such time as you may wish to bestow them on a brother or sister who needs the strength of your friendship and your solidarity."

Back then some of us wore beads all the time. If we saw a friend who was deeply troubled, or worried, or mourning the loss of a loved one, we'd take our own beads off and place them around the neck of our friend. One friend of mine told me years later that he is still deeply moved when he remembers this transfer of beads from my neck to his. Some of our older children were also into wearing beads at that time.

Chapter 12

Summer Home in Vermont – Our Ninth Child

Kahlil Berrigan Cappuccino *arrived in 1970. He was named for three people: Kahlil Gibran who wrote "The Prophet", and Daniel and Philip Berrigan, Catholic priests who served prison sentences for opposing the American slaughter in Vietnam.*

When our American Unitarian friends, Charlie and Hilda Mason, came to visit us in Pointe Claire and we mentioned we had nowhere to go during summer vacation, they said, "Why don't you come down to our 600 acres of woods in northern Vermont?" We took the three-hour drive. Down the road from their farm house was an abandoned house with a leaky roof. They were happy to let us have it, and to let us buy a few acres around it. We had another of those reverse arguments about how much to pay. They said, "We bought this place for $25 an acre, and we won't take a penny more." It was worth, by then, $200 an acre. After considerable bickering, they agreed to sell us 17 acres at $37 each.

This ancient house in Vermont had been built of hand-hewn 30-foot beams, eight inches square. Clearing out the rubble, we found old green-tinted bottles and some newspaper dated 1863. Before moving in we would have to deal with the resident porcupine.

The next summer all of us, including two-year-old Tran, went to Vermont, and lived in the Mason's house while we worked on making our Jelly-Bean Manor [15] liveable. We were competing for ownership of

[15] Porcupine droppings are the size of jellybeans.

the house with the current porcupine who lived there. We made some repairs and moved in. The second floor was habitable. At the top of the stairway was a door that we could close against the demons of the night. One night a thunder storm drummed against the roof, which we had repaired fairly well, with only a few drops seeping in here and there.

About midnight Robin woke up, took a flashlight and kerosene lantern to go outside, there being as yet no indoor facilities. Sleepy-eyed, he stumbled toward the door in his bare feet. As he opened the door, he let out a shriek that may have been heard by our nearest neighbour two miles over the hill. He slammed the door so hard that it bounced back open. He tore through the room, tossing the chair with the lighted mosquito candle behind him, leaped onto the table and shouted, "HE'S HERE! HE'S HERE!"

Bonnie screamed; baby Tran cried; I hollered, "WHO'S here?"

"THE PORCUPINE!" shouted Robin.

"DID HE COME IN AFTER YOU?"

"I DON'T KNOW!"

I got the flashlight and looked all around the room and then down the steps, where, sure enough, serenely stood the porcupine three steps from the top. Barefooted Robin had almost stepped on him. Bonnie and I threw plastic cups at the beast, but he was still undecided about whether to go down or up. As I held the flashlight on him, Bonnie said earnestly, "Fred, close the door!" As I hesitated, she said in a quavering voice, "Fred, *PLEASE* close the door!" which I was reluctant to do because we would lose track of him. But I closed the door. I always do what she tells me.

After she noticed a bat flying around inside, Bonnie insisted that we go up to the Mason's house for the rest of the night. I warily opened the door and went down to search out the porcupine. He was resting on a shelf behind the stairs. He was not foolish enough to go out into the downpour. While I kept the light on him, the kids upstairs put boots on over their pyjamas, rolled up the sleeping bags and cautiously descended the stairs. We retreated to the Mason's house, up the road in the rain like refugees, abandoning our house to the porcupine. We lost the battle, but not the war. We later got rid of the porcupine and lived in our ancient house for the rest of the summer.

Annie Laurie at age 11 won a prize for this drawing, earning her a six-month scholarship for art lessons every Saturday in Montreal

One evening Charlie Mason invited Henry, the water dowser, to determine where to dig a well. Henry said, "I need to cut a forked stick. It has to be from a fruit tree." He got one from a choke-cherry tree. The water dowser was somewhat soused, perhaps to help make contact with the liquid in the ground. He said, "My father was able to find water, but none of my brothers can. I'm the only one with the talent."

We all watched as he held the stick out, butt end forward from his ample belly, walking back and forth. After about ten minutes, the butt end started to point down, and he said, "Strong vein! If they drill and find water at less than 100 feet, it'll be $50. If the vein is below 100 feet, you don't owe me nuthin'." Since the level of nearby Flagg Pond was only about 40 feet lower than where we were standing, I thought it was an easy $50.

The water dowser had come in an old Chevy. The next day the well driller arrived in a Lincoln Continental. Three men followed in a truck. They drilled down 150 feet (at $7.50 a foot) before they found enough water to make it viable. The well drillers got $1125.00. Old Henry got nothing. [16]

In the summer of 1970 Bonnie heard that the Montreal Children's Aid Society had an East Indian baby to place. Tran was two years old, and Bonnie was desperately anxious lest our house not have a baby. I said, "there's no big rush - no need to interrupt our summer vacation." But she filled out the papers. Bonnie and I got our medical exam in Hardwick, Vermont, and drove up to Montreal to get this lovely baby. Kahlil was three months old, born in Canada of a Canadian mother and a father from Pakistan.

Cappuccino Comments (*Lakeshore Unitarian Newsletter*) Sept 4, 1970:

By custom and tradition the caboose is the last car of the train. It is the end — finish. One can depend on it. I used to think so until I came to Canada and saw a train with four cabooses.

The last caboose in our family arrived in our home on Aug 21. Of East Indian extraction, Kahlil Berrigan is 3½ months old and is our ninth child. I thought we had reached the end four kids ago, but Bonnie never committed herself. "We'll

---

[16] Another tale of dowsing lore was told about Maxville Manor, our local senior citizens home. The lawyers on the board of directors decided to call in the well drillers, who came and drilled several dry holes at considerable expense and then gave up. The farmers on the board suggested that they do it right this time and call in a dowser, which was done. He suggested a spot, and the drillers came back and found abundant water.

see," she would say. But now she agrees that Kahlil is the final adoption, and for her benefit I am hereby putting it in writing...

Of course, baby Kahlil came with us to Vermont. My parents drove up from Pennsylvania one week-end. We had not yet told them about our latest acquisition. They arrived on a Friday evening, registered at a nearby motel, and came over to visit. Since it was getting dark and they were tired, we thought we'd wait until morning to break the news about another baby in the family. So we kept sleeping baby Kahlil in a buggy in a bedroom and asked the kids to keep the secret until the next day.

However, my curious Dad, a builder by trade, was fascinated by this ancient building with eight-inch-square beams. He went into all the rooms. Finally he saw the carriage. He picked up the net and looked in. Then he came out and saw Tran, a little older, but already familiar to him. We were all furtively watching him as he went back and looked into the carriage again. Finally, he said, "Hey, Freddie, ain't that another one?"

The kids all laughed and Bonnie said, "The secret's out." Actually, my parents loved all our kids, but they were anxious lest we overextend ourselves. I was anxious, too - but Bonnie? Never. "It'll work out," she said. The wherewithal came from joint bank account #3077-44.

Several times that summer (1970) on the way to Vermont, we had a hassle at the border. American immigration officials were wary of foreign children. Tran had a Vietnamese passport. One time they actually wanted to confiscate his green card we had obtained at the American Consulate in Montreal. Since we were American citizens, we couldn't obtain Canadian citizenship for Tran. We decided it was time to find a few acres in Canada. Later we became citizens of Canada so that our children could become Canadian citizens.

We saw an ad for land in Ontario for $3000 and we went to look at it with the realtor. He also said he had a 100-acre farm with a log house for sale.

I said, "No point in seeing it - we can't afford $8000."

But Bonnie, raised in Illinois, where Abraham Lincoln had been raised in a log cabin said, "Fred, it won't hurt to just go and look at the log house." We went with the realtor, drove up the quarter-mile lane, passed bales of hay in the fields, and there stood a century-old house, unoccupied for 15 years. Actually, for the realtor the log house was an afterthought. It was the land that was worth something. But while the house had no electricity and no plumbing, the roof was sound and the windows intact. We bought it in August, 1971.

Our log house, built in the 1860s, and our 12-seater van

After we chased out the groundhogs, the house wasn't a bad place to spend two summers while still living in Pointe Claire. The logs were hand hewn and snugly fit. We felt like intruders, staying in a home built of cedar from the land itself by skilled craftspeople, who also cleared the land and piled huge boulders in fence-rows.

Loch Haven looking south. Weeping willows are on the left bank

Ice-covered Loch Haven, looking north. Attached to the house on the right is the Annex which we added, with a frame for the greenhouse. Six boys slept out in the Annex with their own wood stove. In winter they froze. On the pond here, the captain of the tractor inner tube vessel is red-haired Pierre on a visit from Seattle. The girl at the bottom is Pierre's red-haired daughter Rene, now an architect who often travels to India with Bonnie

Here in Scottish country (Glengarry County) we had to have a loch, so we hired a derrick that was working in the area. Loch Haven is now five feet deep, 20 feet wide and 130 feet long - a joy to watch all year round. Every spring we would take the youngest kids, with buckets and window screens, to the local stream to catch minnows - probably against the law - bringing 50 or 100 back to Loch Haven. In the fall the Great Blue Heron would swoop in and devour 93.8 % of our fish crop. Some winters a few survived under the ice and the next spring there were hundreds of tiny baby fish.

**Tran with Buttercup, one of our two Saint Bernards.
The other was Pansy**

Chapter 13

Fifteen Bangladesh Babies – Our 10th Child

Shikha Deepa Margaret Cappuccino *arrived in 1972.*
She is named for the nuns who saved her life – Sisters Deepa and Margaret
Mary. Shikha, her original name, is Hindi for "flame". Shikha is also named
for her great-aunt Margaret Trevis.

In 1971, Bonnie read media reports predicting some 5000 babies
would be born as a result of the Bangladesh war of independence,
fathered by enemy Pakistani soldiers. These children would be classified
as "mixed race" and would be outcasts. Bonnie hoped the Bangladesh
government might allow overseas adoptions and we planned on travelling
there to see if we could bring back some of those babies.

Meanwhile, *Families for Children* received its charter as an official
adoption agency. In this capacity we went to see the first Bangladesh
High Commissioner, Mr Momin, in Ottawa. He said he would write to
Bangladesh on our behalf.

On our second visit he told us he had received word from a
Bangladesh government minister, Rab Chowdhury, that inter-country
adoption had been approved in principle. Mr Momin also gave us the
name of his sister-in-law, Mrs Zahira Rashid, who would help us in
Bangladesh. Donations came in from Anglican, Catholic, as well as
Unitarian groups, totalling $5000. The trip was on.

We found wonderful friends to babysit our seven children and two
St Bernards, Pansy and Buttercup. Bonnie, as president of *Families for*

Children, wrote to all the adoption agencies in Canada. The letter said, in part:

> *We understand that these babies may not be accepted by their mothers or their country, and their only hope for a good life is to be adopted outside of Bangladesh. It is possible that your agency has families already studied who are waiting for mixed-race or minority race babies. We would like to take dossiers of families who are ready to take one of these babies, and bring back these first babies with us. The travel cost for each baby, to be borne by the parents, would be about $500. Families taking overseas children must be unusually committed people who would be willing to accept the children with no guarantees. Of course, the children would have to pass the rather stringent medical test required by Canadian Immigration. There is no guarantee of how light or dark complexioned the child will be, so they should be able to accept a child of any colour.*

Fifteen families were selected from four provinces for 16 babies (Helke and Bob Ferrie wanted two.) Families had to gather 13 documents:

Home Study from Adoption agency
Birth Certificates of Parents (2)
Marriage Certificate
Health Certificates (2)
Letter of Credit from Bank
Letter of Provincial approval
Power of Attorney
Letters of Reference
Pictures of Family
Canadian Immigration paper for child
Medical Report on child

One minor point here is that some months earlier when we were proposing the trip, I had assured the congregation that parenting nine

110

children was quite enough, and that we were not seeking another child for ourselves. Then Bonnie said, "Here, just sign these papers. I'm in a hurry. Don't bother to read them, just sign."

Families for Children was funding Bonnie and me. Liz Mowling, a member of our adoption group, asked if she could come along if she paid her own way. This was agreed and we were glad to have her. Liz's help turned out to be invaluable. We might not have succeeded without her. The three of us left on June 26, 1972. The Ferries would join us later. The return was scheduled for July 19th.

We arrived in Dhaka with loads of baggage, mostly diapers and clothes for the babies Bonnie was certain she would find. The next morning we reached Mrs Zahira Rashid by phone who said she would help us and gave us names of officials in the social welfare branch. We consulted her almost daily on how to approach government officials. Her husband found us space in the less expensive Purbani Hotel. We looked out from the seventh floor on people, carts, shops and mosques. Further out was the river with ponderous sails moving big freight dhows along the horizon.

Bonnie found babies at Shi Shu Bhavan, Mother Teresa's Home, run by the Missionaries of Charity in Old Dhaka. The Superior was Sister Margaret Mary who welcomed us and said she had been expecting us after receiving Bonnie's letters.

She took us upstairs to the baby room which contained 20 neat wooden cribs, painted white. The cribs for very small babies were wicker baskets on stands. A light breeze wafted through the screen-less windows but flies were notably absent. The windows were barred with wooden spindles to keep children from falling out. There were 17 babies, all under eight months of age. One was lying in a primitive incubator and weighed little more than a pound. Bonnie asked if we could help tend the babies. The sister said, "Certainly, and I dearly hope you can persuade the government to let them go to Canada. Otherwise, who knows what will happen to them here. Even with the best of care, they catch cold or infection so easily. There is no substitute for a good home with loving parents."

According to Muslim tradition, women are under severe sexual restriction. If a man other than her husband sexually violates a woman, even against her will, her reputation is irreparably harmed. One official told us of being tied up and having his wife and other female relatives raped before his eyes. The pain of these people was appalling. There was no way these babies would be accepted in the community so the government provided abortion clinics so that mothers could be relieved of an impossible burden. Mother Teresa's nuns were waiting at these clinics. Occasionally a fetus was born alive and the baby was brought back to the Home and nurtured with great care and love. Some weighed little more than a pound. Some did not survive.

In the mornings we visited government officials; every afternoon we tended babies - changing diapers, feeding, and holding the babies. We did not meet Mother Teresa, who was travelling. While we respect much of the work she was doing, we also feel she did a disservice to humankind by opposing artificial birth control.

The Home was a beautiful place. There was a softness in the very concrete itself, smooth and polished. There was an aura about the babies, so fragile, with miniature hands and feet. Some babies were so small they were fed with an eye dropper. The young nuns wafted around in bare feet. The white habits of the Missionaries of Charity nuns are like saris, with blue stripes along the edge of the white material. All of the nuns we met had come from India. Government officials (Muslim) knew about these Christian sisters and respected them. As evening fell, several nuns took a big pot of soup outside the gate to feed hungry beggars. Then the babies were tucked in for the night, and we reluctantly took bicycle rickshaws back to the Purbani. At dusk all the women disappeared. Among the teeming masses of Dhaka, not a single woman could be seen outside after dark.

After a good night's sleep and breakfast over, we were off to government offices. Two Canadians helped us greatly. Father Labbé,

Director of Catholic Relief, graciously allowed us to use his Dhaka office as a receiving place for telegrams, and also let us use his typewriter, copy machine, and telex. The other was Emil Baron at the new Canadian High Commission. He wrote a letter on High Commission stationery introducing us to the Bangladesh government. This letter opened doors for us.

Armed with the letter, we made our way to speak to two government ministers. In front of the offices were vestibules with male secretaries. When we said we were from Canada and wanted to see the minister, we were greeted with broad smiles, "You're from Canada! Please come in! Come in!" Canada was highly regarded by everyone as a peace-keeping nation. [17]

After Bonnie explained that we were hoping to adopt orphan children, one minister said, "That's a wonderful idea! Why don't you adopt me and take me with you to Canada?"

Bonnie laughed at his little joke, and answered, "That's a good idea," and then returned to the subject of adopting children. After he asked questions about it, he promised to do what he could to help.

Another minister was Rab Chowdhury, Coordinator of Relief and Rehabilitation, to whom Mr Momin in Canada had written earlier. He promised to help, and said, "Please don't leave without taking the children." But time was running out.

We had to get everything done by July 19th, our departure date. By accident we ran into a representative of International Social Service. They were trying to gain world-wide control over international adoptions, but tragically their requirements of paperwork and red tape were monumental. During the period that Harry and Bertha Holt were

---

[17] This is no longer true. American students travelling abroad used to put Canadian flags on their back-packs. They felt safer. Then Canada joined George Bush's war against Iraq. The war was based on lies. Canada is now lumped together with the bellicose USA. The result of the bombing is a Jihadist movement that will not go away. You can't just bomb people and expect them to tacitly forgive you. As the prophet said, "For they have sown the wind, and they shall reap the whirlwind..." Hosea 8:7

bringing in 3000 Korean orphans into the USA for adoption, ISS brought in just a handful. Bonnie asked the ISS worker, "How long will it be before you'll be able to get children out of Dhaka?"

"Months. I don't even have a copy machine yet." We didn't tell her about our 12-day deadline to get our babies out.

Babies can't wait. During our brief time in Dhaka, several more babies were brought into the home, but three babies died. This was always a terrible blow to the sisters and to us. One sister said, "You don't get used to it. Each one is a great loss."

We looked forward to the daily tending of the babies with great anticipation. These little ones had such a will to live that it renewed our resolve. Soon after Bonnie first found the babies, she picked out one for us. The sisters had named her Shikha. She was born after a seven-month pregnancy, weighing two pounds. By the time we saw her two months later, she weighed four pounds. Her tiny hands and feet were brown on top and white underneath. Being so little, she slept most of the time. She was the loveliest baby in the world. This created a problem. Liz Mowling was also selecting the loveliest one. It obviously had to be Shikha. As the days passed, Bonnie became more anxious about this. One day she could stand it no longer: "Liz, which baby are you hoping to take?" Liz looked nervous, hesitated, and pointed to Onil, a boy. Bonnie breathed a sigh of relief.

Now Liz looked more anxious, and said, "Which one are you taking?" Bonnie pointed to Shikha. Liz gave a long sigh. To Liz, Onil was absolutely the most beautiful baby in the world.

Meanwhile, unbeknownst to us, back in Canada Sandra was having a heart-breaking struggle with the Ontario Director of Child Welfare, who asked for additional papers. A letter from the Bangladesh High Commission in Ottawa was not enough - she wanted a letter from the Government in Dhaka.

Without the Director's approval the babies could not enter Ontario. She felt it was wrong to uproot these children from their own culture, for "they would suffer culture shock in Canada." But an adoptive baby would have no culture shock whatsoever if it were placed with a couple who would take it to their hearts. Sandra called a friend in the media and told him what was happening. He said, "Let me see what I can do."

The Director of Child Welfare was telephoned by a newspaper reporter, "We understand that you are not going to allow these little babies into Canada. Is that true?"

Then a magazine reporter called, "Is it true that you are actually prohibiting the Bangladesh orphans from coming to Canada?"

After half a dozen calls from news, radio, and TV people, the Director relented and decided she would allow the babies to come to Canada. We were telexed to that effect.

Back in Bangladesh, the patient Mr Bannerjee, of Air India, was shadowing us, waiting to know if we really needed all those plane seats. Bonnie said "Yes, we're going to need them", but I was not so sure.

As the departure date neared, Helke and Bob Ferrie came to Dhaka to accompany the babies to Canada. As a doctor, Bob did the medical examinations required by Canadian Immigration. Bob would ease our minds on the trip home (if we were successful) because some of the babies were so very small and fragile. We would not have successfully completed the trip without the Ferries' help.

Back at the Children's Home, Shikha developed a fever. We were apprehensive about leaving that evening, but Sister Deepa said she would keep close watch on her. The next morning we learned that Shikha had almost died during the night. Sister Deepa had taken off her own crucifix and laid it under the small pillow, and had held Shikha in her arms all through the night until the crisis was over in the early morning. We were grateful to all the sisters, and especially beholden to Sister Deepa. We don't think the crucifix had any magic in it, but Sister Deepa thought so and perhaps that helped to keep her focussed on the baby.

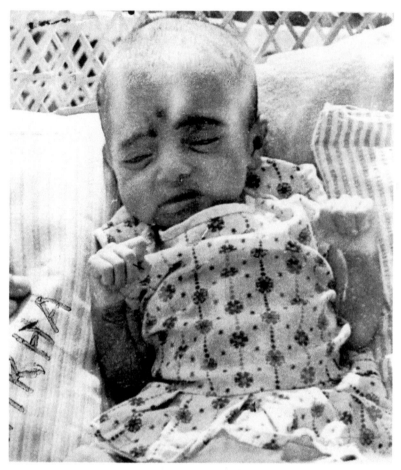

Earliest photo of Shikha

On July 17th, with two days to go, Minister Rab Chowdhury told us, "I have personally made 20 phone calls. The babies are free to go." Whoopee! First we told Mr Bannerjee, "Yes, we still need the seats". We cabled Sandra in Montreal: MAZELTOV, BRINGING 15 BABIES AS SCHEDULED JULY 19 HALLELUJAH.

Bonnie holding Shikha at Mother Theresa's Home in Dhaka.
Liz Mowling is holding Onil, whose little foot is showing in her lap

We still had to go to several offices and answer lengthy questions. One bureaucrat was asking me pointedly, almost angrily, "Did you get the permission from each mother that it was all right with her to take her baby outside of Bangladesh?"

I was really sweating. I lied, "Yes, we have the permissions." We didn't have any such permissions. In most cases the mothers were unknown – and didn't want to be known. I was so relieved when he signed the papers without further ado.

We finally were given *one sheet of paper* with 15 babies' names on it as a group passport, stamped and signed by the appropriate governmental official. The country was new and had not yet worked out procedures for issuing passports. The document stated that the children were being released "*in accordance with the new adoption law about to be promulgated,*" an extraordinary instance of children's lives taking precedence over paperwork.

Bonnie looked at the combined "passport" for the babies, and said, "Fred, the children are going to different provinces and different families. You're going to have to make individual passports for each one."

"How can I ever do that?"

"I don't know - that's your department. Just do it."

So with my propensity for skulduggery and intimate knowledge of forgery, I went to work. I photocopied the single page 15 times, and pasted each individual baby's photo on his or her own copy, highlighting the individual name on that paper. Voila! Each baby had a passport. Actually, they looked quite professional.

On the last day there were tearful goodbyes at Shi Shu Bhavan as some of the sisters bade farewell to the babies whom they had rescued literally from the jaws of death. Other sisters were helping us carry the babies to the airport. The Red Cross provided two vans with drivers. We made it just in time. We climbed the steps to board the plane, the sisters and ourselves holding the 15 babies. The sisters, with tears in their eyes, helped the babies get settled, two or three into each of our laps, and then quietly slipped away.

In New Delhi where we were changing planes, Mr James George, the Canadian High Commissioner for India, met us at the airport and took us all to a big room where we could do the immigration work and also have a rest until time to board the flight to New York. Some Canadian embassy spouses graciously offered to watch the babies in another room, a welcome break for us.

Mr George introduced us to a Canadian immigration official. After greeting and chatting a little, he asked, "May I please have the children's travel documents?" When I proudly handed him my fifteen home-made copies of the single sheet stamped by the Bangladesh Government, he gave me a sober look and said, "These are NOT travel documents."

Mr George assured us: "I'm sure these fellows will find a way to get you all into Canada." The official valiantly busied himself with making papers that would suffice. After some writing and stamping of papers, he wished us well.

From New Delhi, in addition to the five escorts (Mowling, Ferries, Cappuccinos) we had to hire two stewardesses, enough to enable us to care for 15 babies. As we boarded the huge Air India 747 aircraft for the fourteen-hour flight to New York, we prayed that the delicate babies wouldn't become ill. We requested the pilot turn down the air conditioning so as not to endanger the babies. He did.

A woman passenger came forward and hesitatingly asked, "May I hold a baby?"

Bonnie said, "Here. Bring him back if he gets hungry or needs to be changed." Other passengers came forward as well, so the healthy babies were loaned out in kind of a baby library system. As we approached New York the stewardess told us we had to go through U.S. Immigration. We hadn't expected this hurdle because we had been in touch with the American Embassy in Dhaka. She gave us forms to fill out. Since there wasn't time to gather up all the babies and diapers, bottles, etc., and fill out all those papers individually, I quickly wrote the fifteen names down on my own form as my own family.

In New York we were separating. Bob and Helke Ferrie were taking eight babies to Toronto, and Liz and Bonnie and I were taking seven to Montreal.

But we had to take the 15 babies through U.S. Immigration. Each of us carrying two or three babies hurried to the U. S. Immigration counter. The official stopped us dead. He looked at my form with 15 names on it and said, "Are these all your own children?"

I said, "Well, not exactly," and explained that we ran out of time, etc. He wouldn't let us through unless we filled out the 15 papers separately. I said we weren't staying in the U.S., just transferring planes, and there wasn't time. He called his superior in charge of immigration for that airport.

The superior, a huge man of stern visage said, "You have to fill out the papers." Bob Ferrie started to argue with him about jeopardizing the babies' health, and I tried to calm Bob down.

Finally the officer bellowed, "Go on through! Hurry up before I change my mind!"

Bob shouted, "Hurray!" and almost hugged him. We all hurried through, hardly stopping for goodbyes as we split up and headed for the two waiting planes where we were met by groups of Air Canada employees from Toronto and Montreal who had volunteered to come to New York on their own time to help out. What a welcome sight they were. They helped carry babies and equipment up the steps of the Air Canada planes, and travelled with us to Montreal and to Toronto. We were exhausted, but buoyed by the feeling that the babies were almost home.

As the plane taxied toward the Dorval-Montreal terminal a stewardess looking out the window quietly noted, "There are the limousines." Sure enough, a Royal Canadian Mounted Police car with red and blue lights flashing, and three limousines with yellow lights flashing, were waiting to take us to an airport lounge.

Sandra had arranged for the parents to be waiting at the Montreal airport to receive their babies. We dressed the babies in the tiny pyjama suits we had carried all the way from Canada. We put a little red spot on each of their foreheads. This "bindi" is a cosmetic mark used by some people in Southeast Asia who believe it will ward off evil for babies. In pyjama suits of yellow, pink, white and blue, there was an exotic carnival mystery about their appearance. There were enough Air Canada helpers so that we each carried only one baby down the steps and into the limousines.

As we slowly entered the hallway leading to the lounge we saw the television cameras and the flash bulbs popping. It was a joyous occasion as we gradually worked our way in. Immigration officials were there to ease the entry of the tiny new immigrants into Canada. We met Sandra with a big hug and presented her with her baby, Rajiv. She cuddled him and talked to him, the words pouring out of her, so glad was she that the tension was over and the babies were safe at last. Holding Rajiv close to her, Sandra brought forward the other couples. Each couple received their baby. There was no hurry. The immigration officials waited patiently until the parents were ready to bring their baby to the desk to be made a Landed Immigrant of Canada.

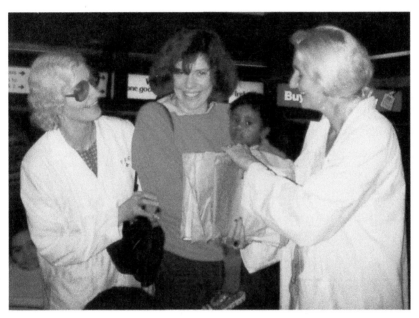

Bonnie and Sandra in white coats were invited by Canada Immigration officials to go behind airport security to assist matching planeloads of children with the correct parents

Even the reporters were caught up in the euphoria. They had tears in their eyes just as the rest of us did. What greater gift can a family receive? The babies are more valued than "the gold of Ophir, …the precious onyx, or the sapphire." [18]

Bonnie talked with each couple, telling them a few trivial things about their child and some details for its care and feeding. Some couples

---

[18] Job 28:16.

had lots of questions. She took time to respond. She would also be in touch later with each family.

We talked with Sandra again and with the others who had helped with the thousand details on the Canadian side. As Bonnie was giving her another hug, Sandra jokingly said, "About this guy, 'Mazeltov,' in your cable who was bringing in the babies…" When I asked Naomi if she knew who Mazeltov was, she laughed so hard she cried and told me, "Mazeltov means Congratulations!"

After we talked to the couples, one French Canadian couple came up to us quietly. They had been admiring their baby for a long time. The father, in half a whisper said, "We don't want to cause any hard feelings among the other families, but we wonder why you chose *us* to be given the most beautiful of the children?"

Bonnie smiled and said, "She is beautiful, isn't she? And now she is in good hands."

Each of the parents felt their baby was the most beautiful baby in the world. But Bonnie and I knew WE had the most beautiful baby in the world.

We shall always love Bangladesh, ever since they made this extraordinary decision to put children's lives before red tape. [19]

After the fifteen Bangladesh war-babies were brought to Canada, Bonnie and Sandra returned to Bangladesh and set up a *Families for Children* Home in Dhaka for orphans and destitute children. They rented a

[19] A more complete account of the 15 babies can be found in the excellent book, PICKING UP THE PIECES, 1971 War Babies Odyssey from Bangladesh to Canada, by Mustafa Chowdhury, 2015, www.xlibris.com. The book includes a photo of our 15 babies. The one error Mustafa makes is writing that International Social Service helped us. Actually they tried to torpedo our effort, but happily failed to do so.

large facility (not large enough), hired caregivers, cooks, watchman, etc. Many of the children had no family and were free to be adopted if the paperwork could be done. Bonnie and Sandra would visit the Home several times a year to make sure everything was going well. Hundreds of children from this Home went to Canada and other countries to be adopted.

The landlord had set a limit of 200 children: "No more than that," he said. "The building cannot accommodate more children than that." But it soon filled to capacity. Reluctantly, Bonnie and Sandra set a firm policy of "No more children."

The *Families for Children* Home in Bangladesh. It had a wall in back which surplus kids could slide over and hide behind

We had a young Canadian volunteer there. One day a teen-age mother brought her tiny infant to the gate along with her own mother. The teenager quietly pleaded (in Bengali), "Please, *please* take my baby. I can't afford to feed him and he will die."

The gatekeeper told them, "We're really so very sorry, but the place is filled. We have absolutely no room."

The mother was desperate, and asked to speak to the manager of the Home. The young Canadian came out. He heard their urgent request through a translator. He said, "I'm aware of your plight, and I really sympathize with you, but our landlord won't allow us to take even one more child." When this message was translated, the young mother took her baby a little bit roughly by the neck and proceeded as if to strangle him.

The Canadian screamed, "Okay! Okay! - we'll take him!" So the Home had one more child, and the two women left for an uncertain future themselves, bereft of their beloved and beautiful offspring; bereft of a major part of their future, for grown children are their only pension plan

Although the landlord's limit was 200, the Home soon housed about 300 children. On one of Bonnie's and Sandra's visits they heard of the way children took action when the need arose: at certain times an emergency procedure kicked in. When anyone spotted the landlord coming on one of his routine visits, they would quietly spread the alarm and a hundred of the older children would quickly and silently slip over the back wall of the compound, where they skooched down until the landlord left and the All Clear was quietly sounded. Actually the landlord was a good guy. Anyone who would entrust his property to 200 children has to have a profound sense of citizenship.

Some years later the Bangladesh Government decided they didn't want their Muslim children going into Christian homes overseas. Tragically for the children, all overseas adoptions were stopped. A strong cultural link between Canada and Bangladesh was severed as well, although the Home was still maintained by *Families for Children*.

Chapter 14

Last Year in Pointe Claire – Two More Children

Lakshmi Bic Nellie McClung Cappuccino *arrived in 1973. Nellie McClung (not a relative as far as we know) was one of the first feminists of Canada. Bonnie's maiden name is McClung. Lakshmi is the Indian Goddess of Wealth and Prosperity. Bic was the child's name in Vietnam.*

Tibiki Nimki Jane Eyre Cappuccino *arrived in 1974. The Aboriginal words, loosely translated, mean "Great Thunderbird Woman of the Night". Jane Eyre, one of our favourite heroines in English literature, was reared in an institution and overcame terrific odds to become a truly liberated person.*

After a summer (1972) on our Maxville farm, bought as a summer home, one thing was certain: we dreaded going back to Montreal pollution. Increasingly, we were tempted: "Wouldn't it be fantastic to live on the farm permanently? How can you have lots of kids, own a farm, and not live on it?" In 1973, after much soul-searching, we made the big decision.

Mohan, Kahlil, and Tran out on Bowling Green

On June 10, 1973, the minister's column in the church newsletter announced that I was resigning the next May first.

…We have never had a happier relationship with any congregation, but the farm is calling us.

The June 10th church newsletter had another announcement:

Hopefully, by the time this is read, Lakshmi, eight years old, will have arrived from Saigon. She is part Vietnamese and part East Indian. My wife assures me that this will be the last child we will acquire.

Lakshmi was born in the city of Danang in Vietnam. We know very little of her parents, but she brought a picture of her Vietnamese grandparents, who seem refined and gentle. They were getting older and were concerned about her future after they died. They learned of an American nurse in Danang who was finding adoptive homes abroad for

126

orphaned children. Lakshmi and her grandparents went to see her, and after much careful consideration the grandparents reluctantly decided that being adopted overseas would be the best course to follow for the child's future.

They asked the nurse to find a good home abroad for her. Lakshmi said good-bye to her loving grandparents and was taken to Saigon and turned over to Rosemary Taylor. Lakshmi was unhappy in the orphanage. She was homesick for her grandparents and Danang. Rosemary made special efforts to put the adoption through quickly so she could leave the orphanage and be back with a family again. She had been referred to us because she was thought to be part East Indian. Later we learned that her paternal ancestry was probably African American rather than Indian. Lakshmi was unusually intelligent, and had been writing poetry in Vietnamese.

Lakshmi soon after she came to us, wearing her lethal boots

Just before Lakshmi left Vietnam, she was given a scrap book we had prepared and sent over for her with pictures of our family and our house at 10 Bowling Green. Rosemary later told us that Lakshmi was enthralled, and couldn't believe that some of the long-haired kids were boys. As she looked at the picture of Pierre and his long red hair, she laughed out loud and asked, "Him guy? Him really guy?"

After she arrived, our family took on a different tone. We were all treated to an omelette the next day. Into our big frying pan she poured not only eggs, but rice, tomatoes, and lots of curry. Quite good after you got used to it. She knew only a few words of English, but was clever at sign language. She often cooked fried rice for everybody. Because she couldn't say the names of the spices, she would point to what she needed on the shelf and Bonnie would reach them for her. Lakshmi would smell them to verify, then she would use them skilfully, if a little generously.

Since she was an older child, we gave her the choice of keeping "Bic" as her first name, or "Lakshmi" as a first name with Bic as a middle name. After we explained that Lakshmi was the goddess of wealth, she chose the latter. She had been given some costume jewellery as a going-away present by an American woman in the orphanage. Those items she treasured. Soon after she arrived in Canada she wanted fingernail polish, make-up, and more jewellery. She wore all these as accessories with the tight jeans and high-heeled boots she had brought with her. With the latter she threatened karate mayhem if her brothers annoyed her. After numerous complaints from Tran and Mohan, Bonnie told her she couldn't keep the boots anymore if she hurt people with them.

When she arrived, she was as thin as a bamboo pole, and we were concerned for her health. But she was also as strong as a bamboo pole, and full of vitality. With a mischievous smile, she continually pestered her four older brothers, Robin, Pierre, Michael and Mohan.

Mohan

Lakshmi at age eight, and Tran, age five, both weighed 42 pounds, but she was a head taller. When scrapping on the grass or on the floor, they were evenly matched. She spent the latter part of the summer of 1973 on the farm with us, adjusting to a new life in Canada. Lakshmi enjoyed life immensely. Both she and Mohan, who was slightly older, had very long hair. As they ran about in shirts and jeans, playing soccer with the other kids in the cow pasture, the only way to tell them apart was that Mohan was the taller of the two, and not quite so skinny.

When Bonnie took Lakshmi to a Vietnamese store in Ottawa, Lakshmi bought some ghastly-smelling Vietnamese fish sauce, which didn't help her popularity at the table as she put it on her food - until Vinh Hai, also from Vietnam, came to live with us for a while. He loved the fish sauce. One day, after I had become a vegetarian, I poured a little on my rice. There was an immediate gleeful outburst from the kids, "Ha Ha on Daddy!" I had thought it was sauce to *put on fish*. But they told me it is sauce *made of fish* - anchovies. So our St Bernards enjoyed a little extra tasty rice that evening.

Lakshmi's language was picturesque as she mixed in a few French words she had learned in Vietnam: "Somebody boku" meant "everybody." Also she put some of her clothing in a box and labelled it "Lakshmi Clots." The kids then would say "clots" when talking about

129

clothes (as in: "Michael, don't leave your clots all over the floor.") She didn't know what "swim suit" meant, but when one of the boys said "bikini," she repeated, "Ah, bikini!" and understood. One time when a friend invited her to "go sledding", Lakshmi started dressing to go to a wedding.

She was fascinated with books. She had brought several Vietnamese books with her which she used to pore over. In one, a photo caption showed that it was *Silas Marner*. Since she could read her language, she retained fluency in it for over a year, longer than did most of our other children. They tended to lose their original language in about six months, which was the time needed to learn to speak English. Bonnie's weekly visit to the library had to include a dozen books Lakshmi would pick out for herself, mostly Harlequin romances. Lakshmi started school in kindergarten, (Cedar Park School in Pointe Claire) and as she learned English, she advanced in a few months to Grade 3.

Although she carefully maintained her feminine image, Lakshmi rode our new horse, Ben Bolt, showing off to her brothers who were leery of the lively lamentable beast. Ben Bolt was a small skinny horse who didn't know how to walk. He was a trotter. One day he trotted Lakshmi through a barbed wire fence. She had to have stitches on her arm, but the horse survived okay. We sold him.

Later on we borrowed a much bigger, but more gentler horse named Juanita. She was a feminist. Lakshmi could ride her, but when Pierre or Michael tried to ride her, she would just get down and roll over! Luckily they were able to jump clear without getting hurt. Juanita was blind in one eye and once almost stepped on Shikha in her little white snow suit, who had slipped on the ice near her. We then got rid of Juanita, too.

In Pointe Claire in the week before Valentine's Day, five-year-old Tran came home from Kindergarten singing:

When you give a val-en-tine
That's the time for fun, fun, fun.
Slide it under-neath the door,
Ring the bell and run, run, run.

Kahlil, age three, didn't say anything, but pondered this song in his heart and waited patiently for Valentine's Day. When the day arrived, he asked, "Is this Valentine's Day?"

His mother said, "Yes, Kahlil, it's Valentine's Day."

He said, "Good," and went into the front room. He came back to the kitchen, then to the front room again. He went back and forth many times, and by 8:30 a.m. he was beginning to lose his patience. Bonnie asked him what the matter was. With some urgency he took a breath and said, "I'm waiting for the valentine people to put a valentine under the door and run, run, run."

Bonnie explained to him, "That's just a song, Kahlil. It doesn't *really* happen that way."

Little Kahlil looked up at her, frowned, and with hands on hips stammered forcefully, "You don't know *anything* about Valentine's Day," and stalked off.

He kept looking at the front door, getting more and more bothered: "When are they going to bring the valentine?" he demanded of his Mother, who up to this point in his life had provided fairly well. She had been a good mother to him. She thought of a plan of action. She went upstairs and found some extra valentines in a drawer. I took three cards, one each for Tran age five, Kahlil age three, and Shikha age one and signed them: "from the Valentine People." I went out the back door, hurried around the house and slid the valentines underneath the front door. Then I rang the doorbell and ran, ran, ran back around and came in through the kitchen door. Bonnie and I casually strolled into the front room just in time to see the three children opening their valentines. They weren't really curious to know who had brought the valentines, they were just satisfied that their unbearably long wait of two hours was rewarded, and the world was unfolding as it should.

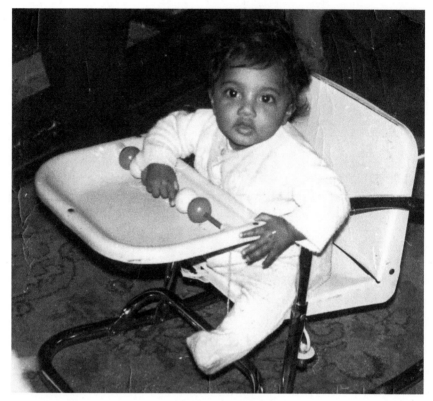

Shikha, age one

In our back yard at Bowling Green was a huge elm tree with a trunk almost four feet across. During the summer, the kids built a tree house, six feet up from the ground. They got lots of practice sawing and hammering. Some kids may have fallen out, but they survived. Mohan was especially adept at swinging himself up into the tree house.

Our two St Bernards, Buttercup and Pansy with Michael (top left), Pierre, Kahlil, Tran, Shikha on Bonnie's lap, Fred, Mohan, Annie Laurie

The minister's column in the April 7, 1974, *Lakeshore Church Newsletter* had the following:

For Unto Us Another Child Is Adopted. Our twelfth child is six years old. She comes from Canada's Northwest Territories, of Ojibway Indian background...Tibiki has brought great joy to our home, and will surely be our final child.

Tibiki soon after she came to us

Bonnie gave her a name somewhat opposite to her apparent diminutive nature. Tibiki was a quiet, resourceful child. She was good at finding things, such as lost rabbits or lost keys. We had Tibiki only a month before we moved permanently to the farm. She said hardly a word - just gazed intently with her big brown eyes. Unlike some of our other kids, she immediately did what she was asked to do. A mysterious child, she seemed to look at things with a different perspective from other people. Soon after we moved to the farm I was talking with her as she stood on the hay wagon, her arm on my shoulder. She said, "Daddy, I'm going to work hard so maybe I can *stay* here."

I was totally melted. A ball came up into my throat. I gathered her little frame into my arms and hugged her for a long time. Slowly recovering from the immense tidal wave of the moment, I explained to her: "Mommy and I love you, and we want you to stay with us - *no matter if you work hard or not - no matter if you are good or not.* That doesn't matter. We love you just the way you are, and I guess you're stuck with this new Mommy and Daddy until you're grown up. Then you can decide what you want to do."

But she worked hard anyway.

One February an alert social worker and close friend in the Social Welfare Department of Ontario informed us that there was an upcoming meeting of all the Provincial Directors of Child Welfare, and that some of them were hoping to remove the privileges of private adoption agencies by forcing them to consult every step of the way with International Social Service (ISS).

This would be a death blow to *Families for Children's* adoption program because the red tape of ISS is monumental and nothing would ever move forward. We had to act quickly. We sent the following telegram to the premiers of the ten provinces as well as to Prime Minister Trudeau:

SOME OFFICIALS AT FEB 28 OTTAWA CONFERENCE OF PROVINCIAL DIRECTORS OF ADOPTION WANT TO DISQUALIFY FEDERALLY INCORPORATED FAMILIES FOR CHILDREN INC, THE FOREMOST CANADIAN GROUP BRINGING ORPHANS FROM OVERSEAS AND WANT EXCLUSIVE PRIVILEGES FOR BUREAUCRATIC MOSSBOUND INTERNATIONAL SOCIAL SERVICE. PLEASE INVESTIGATE AND PREVENT IMPENDING DUAL TRAGEDY OF ORPHANS WAITING ABROAD AND PROSPECTIVE ADOPTIVE PARENTS IN CANADA.

REVEREND AND MRS FRED CAPPUCCINO
LAKESHORE UNITARIAN CHURCH
10 BOWLING GREEN PTE CLAIRE H9S 4W1 QUE

We received responses from Premier William Davis of Ontario and Premier Robert Bourassa of Quebec saying they would look into it. I imagine they did, for ISS failed to gain the sought-after authority. Later on we met one of the participants of the conference, the Director of Social Affairs of Quebec, who told us, "The telegrams caused a bit of a stir, but I was pleased to learn a new English word I hadn't heard before: 'Mossbound.'" (Her first language was French.)

Chapter 15

"Back to the Land," – Our 13th Child

Vodinh Nhat Hanh Cappuccino *arrived in 1975. Vo Dinh was a Vietnamese artist and author who was active in the peace movement. Thich Nhat Hanh is a Buddhist monk also active in the struggle against the Vietnam war.*

A farmer couple holding Shikha. We added this elegant stone porch to our house

We had already spent two summers at our farm. We moved out there for good on May 1st, 1974. Our quarter-mile lane was covered with snow in six-foot drifts. We paid John Archie, our neighbour, to plough out the lane. The log house had about half the floor space of the one at Bowling Green, so a lot of stuff had to be stored in the barn, in the bee house, the chicken house, and the great outdoors.

We bought the tractor, mower, rake, baler, plough, wagon, etc. from the former owner of the farm for $3600. It was a bargain. For years, as long as we had cows, we baled our own hay, about 600 to 1000 bales each summer. One cow needed about 200 bales to keep her through the winter, so we had plenty.

Kahlil, age four

At age four, Kahlil had long wavy hair that bounced on his shoulders when he walked. His favourite pastime when the older kids were in school was to go out into the pasture. If a cow was lying down, he just leaned up against her, listening to the cud churning and gurgling. He informed us if their water tank was empty; or if the electric fence wasn't working; or if two cows were mounting each other in a manner that showed one was in heat. Kahlil would come in and say, "We have to call the Eastern Breeders." And they would come with their artificial insemination equipment.

Kahlil sizing up Mavourneen

At this point some of our older kids, Machiko, Robin, William, and Annie Laurie were already out on their own. We had eight kids at home (by age): Pierre, Michael, Mohan, Lakshmi, Tibiki, Tran, Kahlil, and Shikha. Our neighbours were taking bets as to whether we'd last the winter.

We acquired a pony, with soft grey hair. Bonnie named her Grey Lady. I tried to teach her who was boss (the pony - not Bonnie) but she already knew who was boss (as did Bonnie), and dumped me off her rump in a hurry. Grey Lady was wont, once a year or so, to leave our farm and disappear. We would get a phone call that she was at a horse farm three miles away in Dunvegan, or kindly tied to a fence along the road. One time I went to fetch her and with considerable difficulty loaded her into our van to bring her home. She was just small enough to fit inside. I was driving slowly, steering with one hand and holding the reins near her mouth with the other. As I slowed down at a curve, she budged forward, her head barely touching the windshield. It was just enough to crack the glass. The new windshield cost four times as much as the pony. I should have put a seatbelt on her.

Tran nuzzling Grey Lady

Eleven months later we were the surprised proprietors of a beautiful new-born white colt, standing under his protective mother.

That summer our 55 day-old baby chicks arrived at the Maxville Post Office. With several corrugated cardboard cartons I made a lovely incubator box for them with a light bulb to keep them warm. All this was set on newspaper in a room upstairs where there were no drafts. Lakshmi spent a lot of time watching the chicks.

At bed time it was sometimes difficult to get this gregarious kid settled for the night. When the kids went to bed, the boys would sometimes talk for a while. Lakshmi wanted to do the same and used to sneak into the boys' room. At this time we were lenient with her because, after all, she had many adjustments to make - new country, new language, new foods, etc. But in the boys' room, she teased them so much that there was a lot of noise and we were afraid the babies might be awakened. So I would holler up, "Time to sleep now - no more talking - get into bed."

One night, after hollering up a few times to no avail, I betook myself up the stairs and looked into Lakshmi's room. She wasn't there. So I looked into the boys' room. The three boys were pretending to be asleep. I didn't see her in there so I said to myself, "Ah, she's hiding in the baby chicks' room." I went over to that dark place and sternly said, "Lakshmi, I'm very upset with you for being out of your room..."

No answer.

I said, "You'd better come out! Right now!"

There were stifled giggles in the boys' room. Finally they couldn't hold it in any longer, and they all burst out laughing. Lakshmi had been hiding under a bed. As she crawled out I said, "What are you laughing at?"

She said, "Daddy holler at baby chicks." and she and the boys doubled up with laughter.

One time Tran decided he had had enough of his stupid parents and he would run away. He packed his suitcase and threw his sleeping bag over his shoulder and took off down the lane. Bonnie said, "You'd better follow him, Fred, you know how unpredictable he is." So I sauntered off, keeping a discrete distance. As he rounded Baltics Corners, a kilometre away, John Archie drove by, smiling. He always knew these city folk were a bit weird. As I got closer and could see Tran was tiring. I asked him, "Do you want me to carry the sleeping bag?"

He said (still angry): "No – take the suitcase," which I did. Then I asked if he had anything to eat with him. He said no, and I suggested we go through Ron's orchard, a short cut back to our house. The penalty for being a stupid parent was to carry his suitcase home. I think he had his rock collection in it.

Once when I was over at Ron's next door I nibbled some leaves and told Ron, "This will have a lot of little blue flowers on it in a few weeks. Ron called me later on: "Fred, that plant didn't have any little blue flowers on it. It had one big yellow flower." I never did find out what I was chewing on over at Ron's place. Another time Tran told Bonnie, "It's so embarrassing to go anywhere with Daddy. He's always eating people's weeds."

Tibiki and Kahlil on the old wagon seat, on top of a boulder

Bonnie tells the kids when they're driving to "keep your eyes on the road!" As a high-schooler our son Michael was deeply into cars. In fact, the field on our farm where the "crop" grew best was the field where more and more cars seemed to sprout from the earth. One day he was towing a dilapidated rusty junk-heap up the lane. He told me, "Daddy, I got a terrific bargain. Only a hundred dollars! All it needs is an engine and a little body work." I kidded him about his field of old cars until - I was driving a little Honda at the time, and the engine conked out. He said, "Daddy, I've got a matching engine out in the field; just give me two days." In two days I was driving a rejuvenated Honda, so I didn't kid him anymore.

One day he asked his mother to tow another old clunker to our home from Dunvegan Village three miles away. Bonnie drove him to Dunvegan. He attached the tow rope to both cars, got into the clunker and signalled Bonnie to go. She moved out very slowly and carefully, keeping her eyes in front of her ("keep your eyes on the road!"). When she got home, she stopped, and looked in the rearview mirror for Michael. He was nowhere to be seen. So she followed the route all the way back to Dunvegan. A disgusted Michael was sitting in his old car. He was not amused. "But you tied the rope," said his mother helpfully. The second towing attempt was more successful.

One story I didn't know about until recently took place when Pierre was in high school and babysitting for us. Sometimes while he was talking to a girl on the phone, Shikha and Tibiki would noisily tease him. Once after trying in vain to shush them up he put the phone down, picked up Tibiki and then Shikha, and set them on the top shelf of the bookcase. They stayed very still up there until he finished his conversation. Then he brought them down.

In 1975 when Shikha was three years old, a bit too long for her pyjamas, we cut holes for her little bare feet to stick out.

She used to sit on my lap before bedtime. One time she said to me, "Daddy, smell my feet. I put hand cream on them; they smell very sweet," intently shaking her head yes.

"You're not fooling me again this time, are you?"

"No, Daddy, smell them. They smell very, very sweet."

Pushover that I am, I fell for it. I slowly, slowly, picked up her little foot, and took a whiff.

I made a terrible face: "PHTUI! What an awful smell!" She laughed and laughed.

Then she suddenly got very serious and said, "No, Daddy, it's the OTHER foot. I put hand cream on IT and IT smells sweet."

"You're not fooling me this time?"

"Noooooooh," she said, with a musical lilt, "Smell it. It smells very sweet."

So I slowly, cautiously, took up the other foot and smelled.

I made a terrible face: "PHTUI! What an awful smell!". Her convulsive laughter pealed out through the house. She had played another joke on her dad.

And I know the reader won't believe this, but her Daddy was so gullible that she was able to fool him every single bedtime for weeks and weeks.

I wanted her laughter of that moment to last forever, but, as Kahlil Gibran says,

> *"Your children are not your children…For their souls dwell in the house of tomorrow, which you cannot visit, not even in your dreams."* [20]

---

[20] From his famous book, THE PROPHET

We became involved with the "Back to the Land Movement." A farmer let us have 24 laying hens for a dollar each. We got somewhat of a bargain because he said he had too many. We found out why they were selling so cheaply - most had retired from laying eggs. Some actually did lay eggs for us but by the time we paid for the feed, we estimated the eggs cost us about twice the supermarket price. The hens had protected the garden not only from insects, but also from the growth of tender lettuce leaves, which they diligently plucked. They didn't hurt the onions, though. George, our mixed Irish Wolfhound & Newfoundlander took care of that, digging at random as was his wont. One thing I did learn, too late, was that a good farmer can spot a "retired" chicken. For one thing, the legs are yellower in colour. I guess if the hen is laying, the yellow "goes into the yolk," and the legs are almost white in colour.

Our good chicken house was 10 feet wide and 30 feet long, insulated with sawdust. One day I saw a dead chicken. Not being a farmer, I didn't know if it had had a heart attack or stroke. Then another one turned up dead the next day, and another the next. I was sure it was George. George was a great dog, but when the kids were rassling, he had a knack of determining the likely winner and would grab the pant leg of the loser - the one underneath. But Kahlil was a great defender of the honour of our animals, and regarding the dead chickens he said with absolute and prescient conviction, "It's not George!"

Our neighbour John Archie laughed and told us to stop blaming George - it was more likely a weasel. Kahlil was right. Mohan took a flashlight one night and actually saw the weasel darting hither and thither fomenting mayhem inside the chicken house. One by one, he malevolently and maliciously murdered all the chickens in cold blood so he could suck their warm blood. One unexpected dividend was that the weasel also cleaned out a nest of rats living under the concrete floor of the chicken house. Shortly after that, I was in the kitchen, sitting by the woodstove reading the paper. Suddenly Bonnie screamed and jumped up onto the table. *THERE WAS THE WEASEL!* Having finished off the chickens, he was in the house looking for blood! Bonnie was so juvenile, the way she panicked. I was much more self-controlled and dignified when I climbed up onto the table.

But the weasel just hurried about, sniffing here and racing there, and was gone. John Archie said weasels are harmless and we should be happy to have one around the house to kill the mice. He's a beautiful creature. In winter his fur changes to all white, except for half his tail, which is black. In his white stage he is known as ermine, which was utilized in the royal robes of European monarchs. One night I was sound asleep when I felt this animal running over my feet! I jumped up so fast I sprained my back. The next morning the kids wanted to know why I was hobbling around. I told them. They thought it was funny. I told them that when the mice are all eaten, the weasel goes after little boys' toes. They still thought it was funny.

On the morning of May 9th, 1975, near the end of the Vietnam War, Bonnie got a telephone call from Naomi Bronstein in Montreal: "There's a Vietnamese baby in Denver who was just air-lifted out of Vietnam. He has a small disability. Do you want him?"

"Do I WANT him!!!" hollered Bonnie, and then the wheels started to spin. 45 minutes after the call Bonnie was leaving for Montreal airport. She flew to New York City, met the baby who had been flown from Denver and had the baby back home the same evening. The baby, with a slight disability, had been brought from Vietnam to a group in Denver who were arranging adoptions to the USA. He was identified by the single word "Bronstein" on his wristband. The people knew Naomi Bronstein and, from the wristband, figured that Rosemary Taylor in

Vietnam was sending him to *Families for Children* in Canada. And because he was disabled Naomi was sending him to Bonnie.

Bonnie accepted him not knowing what his disability might be. It turned out that he was healthy except for chronic running ears. We immediately obtained treatment for his ears, but unfortunately he had already suffered 30% hearing impairment in both ears. Bonnie had applied for a child because there were a lot of children in the orphanage who hadn't been placed yet, and it was urgent to get them out, but we didn't know anything about this particular child. Because of medical problems he was considered hard-to-place. He was with a group of children on a ship sent to Guam. From there he was brought by plane to Denver. He was admitted to Canada *with no papers whatsoever* on the promise from *Families for Children* (FFC) that the papers would follow.

Without a birth certificate, we didn't know Vodinh's exact birthdate. The orphanage said he had come as a tiny infant and he had been there about a year so we figured he was about 14 months old. We took him to Dr Vaidya, our family doctor, who agreed that he was likely born in March of the previous year and suggested we pick a date for his birth. The three of us agreed on the first day of spring, March 21, 1974, to be his birthday.

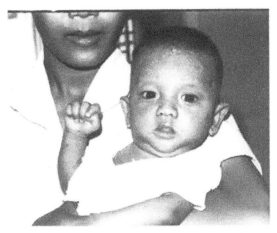

Vodinh on his Vietnamese passport

Near the end of the war, Rosemary Taylor and the other workers were desperately trying to get the remaining children out, and a huge American military cargo plane aided in the transport. In the hurry, as the plane was taking off, a rear door opened on the lower level of the plane. Apparently, many children and some staff were sucked out, fell to earth and died; the plane crashed nearby in a rice paddy - a horrifying event. Many of these children were destined for *Families for Children*, and some of the adults killed were known to us. One was Margaret Moses, a beautiful, caring young woman and dear friend we had known from her previous trips bringing in children.

Time magazine had a cover picture of the fatal crash, showing Naomi Bronstein's agonized face. She was present at the crash site and saw it happen. Lovely Margaret Moses perished with the children she adored.

We were quite upset later on to hear that some of the families who were to receive these children considered initiating a lawsuit against the operators of the plane for damages. These parents didn't seem to realize it was wartime, and the airline personnel risked their lives to try to get as many children as possible out of the country to safety. How could people be so insensitive as to bring lawsuits against them? Everybody had been begging somebody to please do something - anything - to get these kids out.

Some years before, Bonnie, Sandra, and Naomi were seeing Margaret Moses off at Montreal airport after she had escorted a group of children to Canada. They were all laughing, as was their wont, in the coffee shop. The plane was announced, but Bonnie suggested there was time for another round of coffee. Everyone agreed. They didn't want Margaret waiting in a long line. After laughing and telling stories, they finally realized it was getting late, and ran to the gate: "I'm sorry, Ma'am, the gate is closed." Margaret would have to wait a week for the next plane. What else could they do but stand there and laugh their heads off?

Chapter 16

First Sri Lanka Trip

Sandra Simpson, Naomi Bronstein, and Bonnie alternated as President of *Families for Children*. They have all been awarded Canada's top honour: membership in the *Order of Canada*.

The time was ripe to set up an adoption program in another country. The Vietnam program had been abruptly stopped. We were very happy that the Vietnam War was finally over, but we still had many approved families who wanted to adopt children.

The three women and I went to Ottawa to meet Dr Tambiah, High Commissioner of Sri Lanka. He was full of suggestions: "You must visit Mr. So-and-so, a former student of mine who is now a government minister..." We wrote to all these people requesting appointments to meet them in Sri Lanka.

The Gundy family for whom we had previously found a child, agreed to finance the entire trip. Dr Tambiah's son, Gulam Tambiah, a lawyer in Colombo, would help us. At this point, Sandra, Naomi, and Bonnie had a total of almost 35 children in their own three families.

In Sri Lanka in May, 1976, Bonnie, Sandra, Naomi, and I were welcomed by Gulam Tambiah and his charming wife, Mallika. She is Sinhalese; the Tambiahs are Tamils.

Sandra, Naomi, and Bonnie at the Canadian High Commission in Sri Lanka

Gulam took us over to meet his best friend. Fonseka was a smiling young bachelor and astrologer. He arranged marriages and set wedding dates according to the stars and planets. At Sandra's insistence, he started reading palms. He told Naomi she will be in the news in three years (she was always in the news) and that she would live to the age of 71. [21]

He told Sandra she would live to a ripe old age and would be much more effective in her social relationships if she could only control her tongue. She howled: "That's true! That's true!" Actually, Sandra had a special gift for tongue control. Sometimes we would hear her talking on

---

[21] He was wrong. We lost lovely Naomi at age 65.

150

the phone to some pompous bureaucrat. She would gradually lead him into a corner and then draw and quarter the unfortunate fellow.

Fonseka told Bonnie she was a good organizer.

He told them, "Each of you will have even more children in your future – a lot of children. [22]

With Gulam Tambiah's help, we met many government officials, including the President of Sri Lanka, which was a ceremonial post, but we were honoured to meet him nevertheless.

Bonnie and I developed a long-range plan whereby we would return to Sri Lanka with our family and stay for perhaps three years to operate a children's home and to work with adoption officials in Sri Lanka. Gulam introduced us to leaders of the Tuberculosis Association who ran a Home for children from tubercular families. Some were orphans. We also met officials who were doing adoptions and who would like to find homes for these children.

After we got back to Canada, Dr Tambiah took the one-hour drive from his High Commission in Ottawa to visit our Ontario farm. He wanted to see for himself what kind of people we were. I was a little anxious when he stooped his big frame to get into our chicken house that hadn't been cleaned for a while. He met seven of our children and was quite intrigued by the whole adoption practice in Canada. He decided we were ordinary folk and our motives were honourable.

[22] The three women's total number of children increased from about 35 to about 55.

Clockwise from top, Vodinh on Michael, Mohan, Shikha, Kahlil, Tran, Tibiki

With the letters of support we had from political officials in Sri Lanka, and letters from important Canadians, including two from Prime Minister Trudeau, we were confident we would be approved. We were anxious to go to Sri Lanka immediately, but one person had doubts about us. He was the Visa Officer in Dr Tambiah's High Commission office. At one point he stated angrily, "We're going to investigate where this foundation money is coming from, and who is going to benefit!" He seemed to suspect that we had an underlying purpose different from the purpose stated in our project outline.

To help pay for the trip Bonnie decided to sell all our worldly goods. Our farmer neighbour, John Archie, was an auctioneer.

AUCTION SALE
OF ANTIQUES AND FARM ANIMALS
AT BALTICS CORNERS
On Greenfield Road, 2 and a half miles south of Dunvegan
SATURDAY SEPTEMBER 11 (1976)
at 12:30 p.m.

Pine corner cupboard, large pine kitchen cupboard, organ, cradle, 3 kitchen cupboards, 2 rocking chairs antique, 3 china cabinets, antique stereopticon complete with pictures and case, 2 desks, candle holders with globes, pair coal oil wall lamps complete with reflectors, number of dressers, quantity of mirrors, very large bean pot, quantity of old bottles, pictures, frames, dining room table, quantity of gramophone records, 2 antique tables, 5 dining room chairs, book cases, very large quantity of books, antique desk, sad irons, copper kettle, spittoon, 4 cast iron potato pots, antique ink wells, mantle clock, antique glass hen, quantity of crystal, platters, cake plates, silver butter dish, quantity of odd old dishes, cake stands, gal. butter churn, elec. butter churn 3 to 5 gal cap., Magee Pearson, large box stove, 2 small tables, 2 wall cabinets, quantity of chairs, arm chairs, folding arm chair, wringer washer, elec. fry pan, Ind. elec. sewing machine, swivel office chair, 1000 lb. scales, ice box, lanterns, 2 hospital beds, metal filing cabinet, 2 wardrobes, wooden Canada goose, heavy duty elec. stove, food slicer, bicycle, Coleman heater, 3 sinks, wash tubs, quantity of used tin, 3 cow stanchions, bale fork, elec. motors, harness, team britchens new, pony saddle, hay elevator, cattle water tank, hydro elec. fencer, chain blocks, Ferguson front end loader, sulky plough, rubber tired milk wagon, Ferguson snow blower, circular saw, walking plough, car trailer, 130 foot cable. Many other articles too numerous to mention.

Bonnie sold everything: all our furniture, all our electrical appliances, the dishes, the car, every stitch of clothing - even my overcoat: "You won't need that in Sri Lanka."

Our next door neighbour, Ron, agreed to keep in his barn the 1000 books I had hidden from Bonnie. He also rented our tractor and farm equipment.

One item was a carved wooden African statue about a foot high. I explained to the crowd: "This is something I've been trying to get rid of for years, but Bonnie wouldn't let me. It's an African fertility goddess." As the laughter died down, there was brisk bidding for it. I don't remember who got it - some other unsuspecting fellow, probably. Nor do I know whether it worked for his wife as effectively as it did for Bonnie.

We sold our prize cow, Mavourneen. Bonnie had named her after the girl in the old Irish air "Come back to Erin, Mavourneen, Mavourneen...," the Irish Mavourneen was a demure lass with delicate charm. Our Mavourneen was a trouble-maker. Just as I was patting her and telling the people how gentle she was, she got spooked by the crowd and took off right through them, stepping on someone's toe. I pursued her down into the pasture, and heard later that no one wanted to bid on her. John Archie bid and got her cheaply for his own herd.

Bonnie and I felt like the rich young man who was required to "...go and sell that thou hast, and give to the poor..." [23] We felt a sense of loss. But a stronger feeling for both of us was relief to be rid of the burden of all these things.

There was a slight problem in convincing some of the younger kids to go to Sri Lanka, leaving their friends and the old farm. We tried all kinds of arguments about helping the world's children, and the educational value of seeing another country. Nothing availed until I happened to mention that on the plane, if you want a coke, you just push the button and when the stewardess comes, you ask her for a coke. (It worked that way back then) That did it. All seven were ready to go.

[23] Matthew 19:21

Chapter 17

Second Sri Lanka Trip and India

Finally Dr Tambiah confided that we didn't really need a visa. He said we could obtain one-month visas in Colombo when we arrived there. Surely Gulam Tambiah would help us work it out after that. Departure was set for Nov 30, 1976. We packed all our goods in 50 assorted suitcases, cardboard cartons, and feed sacks. A friend, Charlie LeBer, had a large van. First we loaded the 50 pieces of luggage. Then we piled the kids on top of that, leaving just enough room for Charlie to shoehorn in Bonnie and me. This was before seat belts. As we drove to Montreal Mirabel Airport, a blizzard struck. Charlie could hardly see to drive, but we were ever so glad to be out of our one-stove log house.

We were anxious about leaving our 17-year-old Michael and 18-year-old Pierre behind but they preferred to finish high school in Canada, so we arranged for them to stay with neighbouring farmers, helping with chores and riding the school bus to their high school.

After the blizzard in Montreal, it was pleasant to disembark to a balmy 75 degrees Fahrenheit in Sri Lanka. Our young Montreal friend, Peter Freud, had preceded us. He had come overland from Europe, almost perishing of sickness in Afghanistan, to help out as a volunteer. He prepared the way for us by meeting Gulam Tambiah and his wife Mallika, who came with him to the Colombo airport. They weren't sure if we were on the plane until Peter saw the 50 boxes and bags on the conveyor belt. He knew from the baler twine and the primitive cartons that they had to be ours. He and Gulam then had to figure out how to get all of the boxes - plus nine Cappuccinos - into the two cars engaged for us.

The Customs officials were intrigued: "Is all this luggage yours?"

"Yes, it is."

"Are all these children yours?"

"Yes, they are." The situation was so unusual for them that they let the luggage through without opening anything. We got our one-month visas, and again, we were shoe-horned into vehicles. Two boxes contained the *World Book Encyclopaedia*, which was consulted daily.

The first thing on Bonnie's agenda was to visit the Tuberculosis Centre, which we had seen on our previous trip. All the children were still there.

We rented a small unfurnished house by the sea with smooth cement floors. Someone lent us a table and chairs and we slept on our sleeping bags. We hired the old watchman, David, who had been taking care of the house. David was a gem. He helped with the cooking and sweeping, and he stayed there to watch our sleeping bags and other junk while we were gone. He knew some English and could communicate with the children, who liked him.

At our rented house by the sea near Colombo. Top, housekeeper David, our driver whose name escapes us, Peter Freud. Middle, Tran, Lakshmi, Mohan, Bonnie. Bottom, Fred, Kahlil behind Shikha, Tibiki behind Vodinh, with the Bruderhof truck

At one outing, a group of friends took our children down the cliff-side to the river to get a closer look at some elephants bathing. They were watching from a raft anchored to shore. Bonnie and I stayed on top with Mallika. We were looking around at the incredible view when Mallika screamed, "GET SHIKHA!" The group on the raft was so rapt in watching the elephants that they didn't notice that tiny Shikha had fallen off and was wallowing around in the water. They heard Mallika and reacted immediately to pull Shikha out. She was unharmed, but her parents were quite shaken by the experience, full of guilt for not watching her more closely.

Shikha, age five

Gulam spent a lot of time and energy working on our visa problem. It didn't help when an Australian adoption group did something incredibly foolish. They mimeographed a little brochure in Australia for prospective adoptive families saying one could go to Sri Lanka and bribe a certain official (whom they actually named) with a bottle of a particular brand of whiskey, and then one would have no trouble adopting a baby. The Prime Minister of Sri Lanka, Madam Bandaranaike was deeply embarrassed. Sri Lankan officials were livid. Their response was decisive. All international adoptions were stopped, and all foreigners were prohibited from doing any kind of child care whatsoever in Sri Lanka.

Bonnie and I were demoralized about having to leave Sri Lanka after only two months. Our children were sad to leave such great, new-found friends, and our house by the sea. In February of 1977 we flew to Bombay with our 50 pieces of luggage to visit friends for a few days and then continued on to Delhi.

Bonnie with Vodinh at our Home in New Delhi

In Delhi we moved to a guest house in New Delhi run by a Mr Mansingh and his wife. We made our own breakfast, usually of whatever fruit was in season. Mansingh and his family served us the other two meals each day. They were strict vegetarians. We learned to like rice with "pulses," which are lentil or bean concoctions. On Sunday evenings we took our seven children to the Golden Dragon, a local Chinese restaurant recommended by Mansingh. The children were glad to have meat once in a while. We never got sick after eating there which is quite a tribute to the quality of the Golden Dragon.

In New Delhi we had to obtain approval from the Social Welfare Ministry to set up an adoption program and a home for children waiting to be adopted. This often took Bonnie into the office of some bureaucrat for a signature. Sometimes she would have to wait two or three hours. For her the time was not lost. She would sit back and observe the people around her in the office with a smile on her face, immersed in the exotic Indian culture.

We visited several orphanages. At one place in Gole Market we were shown a crib where babies were left anonymously. The crib was built into the outer wall of an orphanage. It was hooked up electrically so that the weight of the baby in the crib would ring a bell inside. By the time the attendant came out the person would be gone. Many babies were received that way.

After two or three months of working with a woman at the Indian Council for Child Welfare (ICCW), we began taking care of some orphan children. We hired a nurse, Ellen Flannery, who had experience with young children. A quiet woman, she had a gentleness and competence about her. She knew all about babies and the types of tropical ailments that were a constant danger to them.

The family living next door had a four-year-old daughter about the same age as our Shikha. They played together and became best of friends. Both being quite headstrong they fought daily. It was Tibiki, age nine, who would mediate and arbitrate and adjudicate until the fighting was resolved.

We found Meadowbrook School, an English medium school, six blocks from our home where we enrolled the six older children. Vodinh was too young. There were uniforms to buy - white shirt, red tie, and grey slacks or skirt. About 30 children were squeezed into a room about one quarter the size of a Canadian classroom. Children had to sit quietly and repeat the rote memorization after the teacher, with no opportunity for discussion or moving around. Mohan was the first to drop out: "I absolutely can't stand it. I won't go." Luckily we hadn't yet bought his uniform. After a few days Shikha, Tran, and Kahlil complained loudly about going. The only two who persevered were Tibiki and Lakshmi. They didn't like it, but they went.

While I was escorting the children to school one day, I saw two little boys coming along. One, about age six, was dressed beautifully in the school uniform. The other, perhaps a year older, was dressed in rags. He was holding the books and lunch bag of the first boy. At the school gate, he gave them to the smaller boy and went home alone. He was the servant boy, not entitled to an education.

The school had a good reputation in the community, but was hopelessly overcrowded. We hired a teenage friend who came over and tutored Mohan in math. He proved to be an excellent tutor so we hired him to tutor our other children in math as well. That was the last formal schooling our children had in India.

During our stay in Delhi we were instrumental in helping 13 children to be placed in good adoptive homes in Canada, the USA, and some European countries. But things were moving too slowly. Then we heard that down south in the city of Coimbatore an Indian man was doing overseas adoptions. After I made an exploratory trip to Coimbatore we decided to move there because we felt our program would grow more quickly.

In December, 1977, nine Cappuccinos piled into a passenger train in New Delhi, behind a steam engine and began a forty-six hour trip to Coimbatore, a city of a half million people in Tamil Nadu, the southernmost state. Sitting across from us on the train was a big moustachioed fellow who stared at us but never smiled.

Chapter 18

Coimbatore, India

When the train arrived in Coimbatore we were anxious to get our 35 pieces of luggage off before the train started up again. The whole family ran back and forth pulling everything out. On the platform, amongst our pieces, was a footlocker that didn't belong to us. As the train started slowly moving, we hurriedly carried the footlocker onto it, slid it into its place under the seat of its sleeping owner, the wild-looking mustachioed fellow, and ran to jump off the train. The giant remained sleeping.

We loaded our things onto a borrowed truck and drove to a house in an idyllic little village called Podanur, seven kilometres from Coimbatore. That was to be our home for the rest of our time in India. Mr Deshpande, in his late sixties, rented us three buildings in the centre of a five-acre coconut grove. The main building had a lot of character, with stucco walls and a tile roof. An East wing and a West wing extended from either side of the central dining room. Each wing had several bedrooms and a bathroom. Our kids stayed with us in one wing.

We had hired a cook, several care-givers, a sweeper, a gatekeeper, and a driver, Dammoderin, for the 20-year-old (1958) Valiant automobile (no rust!). Dammoderin drove and maintained the car and stayed with it when I went into the market.

Nurse Ellen Flannery was set up in the other wing where she would care for any sick children. A second building housed staff and older children. The third building, 30 feet square, was for the babies. We hired a woman named Aleyama as manager. She had contacts with some children's homes, and one day went off on a trip. She returned in a car with seven children, all orphans, from Kerala State. We were finally launched.

We were able to get registered as the *Kuzhanthaikal Kudumpam*, a loose translation of *Families for Children* in Tamil, we were told.

**At the gate of our *Families for Children* Home
in Podanur, near Coimbatore, India**

Coimbatore is a dry area. The tube well on our property seemed to run out of water often, so Mr Deshpande hired a well-driller, who brought in a huge noisy diesel engine and a tall frame that suspended and turned a metal cylinder saw nine inches in diameter and three feet tall. The cylinder revolved and cut slowly into the rock as its weight bore it down. After three feet, the rock broke off and the cylinder was hoisted up, bringing up the rock inside. Before going down again, the bottom saw teeth of the cylinder were sharpened. The worker laid these rock pieces out in a line so he could tell exactly the kind of rock he was reaching. Certain kinds of greenish rock were water bearing. The operation needed lots of water to flush up the grains of rock being ground away. Several oxcarts brought water in tanks from a river a mile away.

Driver, Vodinh, Kahlil standing, and Tran bringing water for the well-drilling machine

Kahlil bloomed in India. He and Tran rode the oxcarts with men who were bringing water for the well-drillers. Sometimes the driver let them drive the oxen. One day Tran came home beaming. The driver had gone to sleep and he had to drive the oxen all the way to the river by himself. Quite thrilling for a 10-year-old.

Tibiki, age eleven, spent a lot of time in the baby house. She was a natural nurse and had a gift for taking care of small children and understanding their needs intuitively. The Hindi the children had learned would now be supplemented by Tamil, an entirely different language, which Tibiki used when communicating with the children. Tibiki and Shikha often spoke a mixture of English, Hindi, and Tamil. Shikha, even when she spoke English, spoke with a thick Indian accent, rolling her "r's".

The Baby House at our Podanur Home. This baby is Goodie, whom Shikha helped care for

One time adventurous Tibiki was walking along the top of a picket fence with metal pickets, pointing up like spears, presumably to scare people like her from climbing it. But independent Tibiki is not easily deterred, so in her sandals she walked, balancing herself along the tips. The inevitable happened - she lost her balance, and jumped free - all except her hand, which became impaled on a steel picket. She tried to pull it off, but couldn't, so she called to her sister, "Shikha! Push my hand off!"

"No!" said five-year-old Shikha, "It's Gross!"

"PUSH IT OFF!!" screamed Tibiki.

164

Finally Shikha screwed up her courage, put her hands under Tibiki's, and pushed the grossly impaled hand off the spear. Tibiki immediately went inside to tell Bonnie, who was on the phone talking to someone in Canada. She had told the kids not to bother her when she was on the phone.

When Tibiki came over to her, Bonnie brushed her aside, and pointed a finger at her to not interfere with the phone call. Tibiki waited for a while, and then pushed her bloody hand towards Bonnie's face. Bonnie screamed into the phone, "I have to hang up now. I'll call you back." Bonnie rushed her to the little clinic around the corner. She was given a tetanus shot. They cleaned the wound and wanted to stitch it, but Bonnie was worried about how clean the clinic was so Tibiki's hand was bandaged. She still bears the scar on the underside of her hand even unto this day.

At seven a.m. one morning in January the bell at the gate rang. A man had come from an orphanage 16 kilometres away. He had two children with him and a note from the director of the orphanage asking us to please take these two children and care for them, a sister and brother aged five and six. They had sores all over their bodies. Nurse Ellen said it was scabies and highly contagious.

That orphanage was probably afraid of a scabies epidemic and was anxious to get rid of these children. First we fed them - a banana, an orange, some bread and peanut butter and some rice, all of which they received without a word. In addition to the scabies, they were suffering from the deadness of spirit that some children in orphanages have. They just sat there, neither laughing nor crying - just staring with their big sad eyes. Sometimes when no one was near they would quietly talk to each other. We put them in the small puja room off the kitchen, isolated from the other children. They had to have separate dishes, clothes, and bedding, all of which was washed separately. As night approached the girl began to cry. One of our workers who spoke her language found out that her ankle hurt. Ellen said, "Scabies, if untended, will get into the joints." After Ellen gave her something for pain, the girl went to sleep.

The doctor came the next morning and suggested that both children soak, morning and evening, in a solution of potassium permanganate, purple-red in colour. We bought two barrel-like plastic tubs, and the children sat down in the solution up to their necks, 30 minutes twice a day. When they emerged, their skin was purple-red. We were able to keep them isolated for only three days. After that they improved psychologically and began running all over, just like the rest of the children, and their "orphanage inertia" disappeared. They laughed whenever we looked at them. We continued the barrel treatment and their sores healed after a few weeks. Later they were adopted by a Canadian couple.

Bonnie, Fred, the District Collector, and Mrs Fowler are entertained by Tibiki, left, and children gathered into the Home

By February, 1978, there were 15 children at our Home besides our own. Eight were tiny infants. They were awaiting the paperwork to be done before they could be sent to good adoptive homes in the USA, Canada, Germany and Finland. By April we had 34 children. We needed staff around the clock, especially for tending the babies. That meant 22 adults. We became very much like a big family. By May our Home was about filled up. When people brought children to us, we took them to the Podanur village police office and had the whole transaction recorded and signed.

We had been gone from Canada about a year and a half, and Bonnie and I were ready to stay another year and a half, but some of our children wanted to go home. Bonnie didn't take them seriously until one evening Tran collared her in our bed room and upbraided her: "I'm not getting any education over here. I want to go back to the school in Maxville with Mrs Ferguson (the principal), and continue my education." For an hour and a half he kept bringing up various arguments and finally Bonnie capitulated. It wasn't Tran's arguments (our children were being very well educated in India) - it was his passion that convinced us to go back to Canada.

Going home, Bonnie didn't want to leave India empty-handed, so from all the children in the centre, she picked out two older boys to add to our own family. (It is harder to find adoptive homes for older boys.) In a weak moment I put my name to the required papers, on condition that these would be the absolute last children in our family.

The elder of the two was a nine-year-old with a flashing smile and an easy temperament, named Vijayakumar, after a famous Tamil film star. We kept that as a middle name and added Ashok, named after the famous king of 269-232 BC. The Ashok chakra (wheel) is represented with 24 spokes in the national flag.

The younger boy, six years old, was named Sonny. We were told that he was found as an infant nursing from his dead mother. He became the darling of the staff because he was one of the youngest, after other babies had been adopted out. We changed his name to Kailash. Bonnie added two middle names: Shantidas and Tagore.

These two boys had to have papers processed before they could leave India and this could not be completed before we were to return home. It was heart-breaking to leave them behind when we came back to Canada. It would be many months before they would re-join our family.

Before we left India we learned that Pierre, after finishing high-school in Canada, took the advice of his two uncles, Fred's brother Bobby and Bonnie's brother Bruce, and joined the U.S. Navy.

Pierre joined the U. S. Navy

Chapter 19

Home to Canada – Five More Children

Ashok Vijayakumar Cappuccino *arrived in 1979. Ashok was a king of ancient India who was first a military conqueror. Converted to Buddhism, he became a compassionate and peace-loving monarch, whose "pillar" is seen on Indian currency.*

Kailash Shantidas Tagore Cappuccino *arrived in 1979. Kailash is the holy mountain from which the sacred Ganges River originates. It is also the abode of the great god Shiva. Shantidas is the name given by Gandhi to the philosopher, Lanza del Vasto. Tagore, the revered national poet of Bengal, bestowed the title "Mahatma" on Gandhi.*

Mahleka Kwelanga Uhuru Cappuccino *arrived in 1980. She was born in Barbados. Mahleka Kwelanga Uhuru loosely translated means "Queen's Happy Laughter of Freedom".*

Mei-lin Yin Yee Cappuccino *arrived in 1980. Mei-lin, loosely translated, is a "Beautiful Bird on a Pond". Yin Yee is her given first name.*

Shan Ho Yin Cappuccino *arrived in 1980. Shan's name means mountain. Ho Yin is his given first name.*

In May, 1978, I returned alone to Canada to get my old job back. I immediately bought a cow and named her Sweet Alice (from the song, "Do

You Remember Sweet Alice, Ben Bolt?") She was just ready to calve. I expected the kids to be home soon to do the milking. After her calf was born, I had to milk her before going to work and again when I got home. I called Sandra, and she reassured me, "Fred, you're going to have to get used to the idea that Bonnie won't be able to get airline seats for her and the seven kids until the busy season is over in the fall." At home the only person I had to talk to was Sweet Alice. She and I discussed philosophy together. She agreed with all my convoluted arguments. What a relief it was when Bonnie and the kids got home six weeks later.

Soon after they got home, Vodinh, age four, was sitting in my lap. Shikha, the girl of the sweet-smelling feet, wanted Vodinh to make room for her to sit in my lap also, but he spread out, preventing her from hopping aboard. So in her confidential six-year-old manner, she put her hands on his knees, looked up at him and whispered to him in Tamil, with the appropriate side-to-side head wiggle. Then he said something in Tamil, and she said something along with the head wiggle. Finally he made the same head wiggle, and actually moved over so she could climb on. I gave them both a hug. They settled this whole complicated matter amicably - and I didn't understand a word of it.

Shikha, Vodinh, Tran, and Kahlil in the tub. Tran is safeguarding the moral sensitivities of the reader

170

Our kids went back to the same school with the same children they were with when they left. One and a half years without formal schooling did them no harm. Tran was amazed that his classmates didn't know the capitols of various countries.

Shikha, Tibiki, Kahlil

In March of 1979 our family went to the airport with great joy and anticipation to greet and reconnect with Ashok, our 14th child. Ashok was enamoured of the trees on our farm, so I took him out to the sugar bush. He was flabbergasted at the size of our acreage. He kept saying: 'Is all this Daddy's farm?"

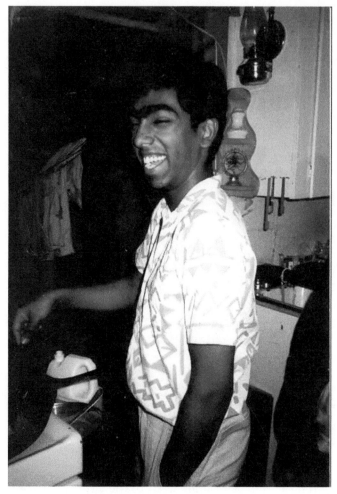

Ashok fit easily into the family

When Bonnie and Sandra went to India in June of that year they brought our 15th child, six-year-old Kailash, back to Canada, along with eight other children for other families. I went with some of the kids to the Montreal airport to meet Bonnie and Kailash. Our kids remembered Kailash from India a year earlier and we all had a happy reunion.

Ashok and Kailash, having gone barefoot all the time in India were able to run barefoot on our gravel lane and on the stubble in the fields after the hay was cut.

One day Tran came home from school exuberant: "Mrs Ferguson (the principal) was telling everyone how kind the Cappuccino children are. Kailash threw up on the bus, and when we got to the school, Tibiki right away ran into the school and got paper towels and came back to clean up the floor, and I took Kailash inside to clean him off. Mrs Ferguson said she was very impressed."

Shikha and Ashok soon after he came to us. Later on they were Head Girl and Head Boy at Maxville Public School

Ashok was taller and heavier than Tibiki, but in her presence poor Ashok manifested a severe disability - he was overly ticklish. Tibiki would chase him around the kitchen table with malice intent. When she caught him he would be totally disabled, screaming and laughing on the floor.

Tibiki was also the one who commented on the floor boards in the kitchen. They were warped from all the water spilled from time to time. She explained to someone visiting that these were "Speed Bumps."

We had a tire swing hanging from a tree down at the maples, about seventy feet from the bee hives. The tire was hung with one of those yellow nylon ropes. Tibiki and her friend Joanna Owen were riding the tire swing. As they went higher and higher, the rope snapped. Tibiki landed on the grass and Joanna landed on Tibiki, breaking Tibiki's right arm. Tibiki landed in the hospital with a pin in her elbow hooked up in traction with a rope and pulley and a heavy weight. What we hadn't known is that yellow nylon ropes deteriorate in the sun.

Some weeks later, when it was time to take the pin out, Bonnie went in and stood at the opposite side of the bed watching the process. Tibiki was talking to Bonnie, and then looked away for a minute to watch what the doctor was doing. When she looked back, Bonnie wasn't there. Bonnie was stretched out on the floor, having fainted dead away. Bonnie always tries to be there for her children when they need her.

By this time I started working at a hospital in Cornwall, as a kind of counsellor to long-term geriatric patients. I would gather groups, serve tea and cookies, and play the autoharp for them. One day I was singing my heart out - I think it was *Beautiful Dreamer, wake unto me* - when one old sister woke up and screamed, "*Will someone* **please** *let that cat out!*" My singing talents were somewhat under-recognized by the music cognoscenti of Cornwall.

A few months later, winter arrived. Our old log house was *COLD*. For twenty-four years, four wood stoves heated the house. The boys used

174

chainsaws to cut the wood from our own woods. When all our 13 sons grew up and left home, Bonnie abjectly refused to go out and cut the wood. Abjectly! I had to invest in oil heat.

Bonnie with her smug smile just got the better of her husband – again – about some issue long forgotten

Sandra's son, Johnny Simpson, stayed with us for a while. One February day, I had dragged Bonnie out for supper, to get away from farm and family. It was then that our Jersey cow Betsy's calf chose to be born. Mohan and Johnny Simpson were assisting with the birth, but there were complications. One front hoof was stuck and Betsy was having trouble, so Johnny called the MacLennans for advice. Norman

MacLennan explained that you have to reach your hand inside, grab the foot, and push the hoof back a little and then it would come out. Johnny did that, and after some effort on Betsy's part, the calf pflooped right out onto the straw-covered floor.

When Bonnie and I got home and heard it was a heifer, I was elated and kept repeating "Oh Happy Day!" over and over. So that's what Bonnie decided to call the calf. It was 62 pounds, large for a Jersey heifer. It was minus 20 Centigrade outside, so of course Happy Day was brought into the house with us. There was no way we were going to chance her catching flu or double pneumonia.

Happy Day remained healthy. We gave her only the allotted litre of milk morning and evening, but she could have all the water she could drink, which was quite a bit. Soon after the feeding, the "rain" would start on a large plastic sheet we had spread out on the living room wooden floor. Vodinh followed her around with a big can, trying to catch as much as possible so she wouldn't wet the floor too much. When told of this, two of my female patients at the hospital laughed 'til they cried. After a week we moved Happy Day out to the annex on the east side of the house. Shortly after that, our second Jersey, Dorothy, also had a heifer calf weighing in at 55 pounds, still above the average for the breed. We named her Carol.

One day Tibiki reported that she and Kailash were keeping warm, sitting on the bench behind the kitchen wood-stove near the loft door. Kailash was experimenting with a loose tooth, poking it with his tongue, but it wouldn't come out. Tibiki suggested, "Why don't you tie a string around it and tie it to the door. When Daddy comes down from upstairs and opens the door, the string will pull the tooth out."

He was summoning courage with two feet of string hanging out of his mouth, when Bonnie came into the kitchen from outside. She had been a little upset with Kailash because he was going through a stage of chewing on the sleeves of his sweaters. "What are you doing with that stupid string hanging out of your mouth?" and she gave it a good yank. She was quite surprised when the tooth came out with it. Tibiki thought it was hilarious, but suppressed her glee because Bonnie was not in the best of moods. Kailash didn't see any humour in the episode, but was glad to be rid of the troublesome tooth.

Our 16th child, Mahleka, left Barbados at age five. She was first adopted by a family from Quebec who had lost a child on the plane that crashed in Vietnam, but the chemistry wasn't right between them and she was referred back to *Families for Children*. Bonnie liked her and selfishly decided to bring her into our family in 1980. She was a cheerful, energetic nine-year-old who fit into our family well. She was happy to participate in all the activities.

Mahleka in school, Nov 1978, before coming to us

One day our social worker, Mavis Nixon, called me at work in Cornwall, and asked if I could come over to see her during my lunch hour. Her office at the Children's Aid Society was just across the street. She was cordial, and said, "Now, about these children from Hong Kong." I guess my mouth must have dropped open, because she said, "Bonnie has discussed with you about these two children from Hong Kong, hasn't she?"

Thinking quickly, as is my wont, I responded, "Well, Bonnie knows a lot more about them than I do," a monumental understatement, as I hadn't heard even the shadow of a hint about this impending earthquake.

First Maxville School photos of Mei-Lin and Shan

These siblings, a girl age 11 and a boy age 10, had been adopted from Hong Kong by a Canadian-Chinese couple. The children stayed a month there and were then moved to another Canadian adoptive home where they remained a year. They were about to be shipped back to Hong Kong when Sandra Simpson heard about it and told the social worker, "Oh, you just call Bonnie Cappuccino." Within the week Bonnie had fetched them from Toronto. They were such pleasant kids and so incredibly good looking that I couldn't understand the agency not being able to find a home for them.

Mei-Lin integrated herself into the family quite well and at the same time kept an eye out for her younger brother Shan, who basked in his new-found freedom of expression. He soon discovered that kids were allowed to use any kind of language they wished – at home, not at school - as long as it was not abusive to someone else, and not when Grandma Cappuccino visited us. Shan's vocabulary blossomed almost entirely into four-letter words.

Mahleka, Mei-Lin and Shan dovetailed right in with the routine of milking cows and feeding calves. The barn chores were done morning and evening. Lakshmi and Mahleka milked Betsy. Mei-Lin and Tibiki milked Dorothy. Shan saw to the watering, and Tran and Kahlil got the bales down from the hayloft to feed the cows and two bull calves (one named Big Blue). When the milk came into the house, Ashok and Shikha fed two and a half pints to Happy Day, and Mahleka fed two pints to the younger calf. Vodinh and Kailash, both age six, made butter by shaking cream in a gallon jar as they watched the limited television that was allowed.

Tibiki always was a skinny little thing. But she used to lord it over the cows. Morning and evening she would go out and order them around, and explain to them that she was the one in charge. I think they believed her. She could get a lot more milk out of them than I could.

I heard conflicting reports about how the shy and diminutive Tibiki behaved on the school bus. Lakshmi reported that there was one bus driver whom none of the kids liked. Tibiki used to throw crumpled paper balls at him while he was driving. It's a miracle they didn't all wind up in the ditch.

Vodinh, age six, was a real joker. When Lakshmi's friends called, he answered, "Hello, who is this? Oh, Jill, are you my girlfriend?" He got a

179

big laugh all around. Then he called Lakshmi to come and talk to her friend.

Each Christmastide we made our pilgrimage to our old Unitarian Congregation in Pointe Claire. One year Tran cut a tree as big as could be squished inside the van, about 12 feet long, for the church. When we got home Tran asked me if I had put a little tin cup near the tree so people could make a donation for the cutter of the tree.

I said I didn't do that, but I did receive $150 from the church.

"For a tree?" asked Kahlil.

"No, not for a tree – for my five minute talk."

Tran calculated: "That's thirty dollars a minute, 50 cents a second. Daddy, if it was me I would have stuttered and coughed a lot."

Clockwise from left, Tibiki, Mohan, Fred, Kailash with Bonnie, Vodinh on Mahleka, Tran, Lakshmi, Kahlil, Ashok, and Shikha

Chapter 20

Vietnamese Boat Children – Our 19th Child

KimChi Cappuccino *arrived in 1980. KimChi is her original name. We couldn't legally adopt her because she had parents in Vietnam, but she was a Cappuccino in Canada until she married Nam.*

Bonnie and Sandra heard of 1500 boat children on an island in Indonesia. They got on the phone and called government authorities in Ottawa, and Ottawa replied, *"Of course, WE can't do anything to help these unfortunate children because it's a provincial matter."*

So they called the provincial authorities in Toronto, who replied, *"Of course, WE can't do anything to help because it's a federal matter."* Now a normal person would let it go at that. But Bonnie and Sandra are quite pushy and overbearing and fanatical when it comes to children, and they would not accept this run-around. Other friends were putting pressure on these governments as well.

Before *Families for Children* could get clearance for 100 children to come to Canada, someone had to guarantee that if the original placement didn't work out, a new place would be found. The local Children's Aid Society didn't want all that responsibility, and certainly the Provincial Department of Health and Welfare didn't want all that responsibility, so guess whose house became an "Emergency Shelter" for Ontario. Sandra Simpson, living in Quebec, also courageously (or recklessly) agreed to take any of the Quebec children who didn't work out at their initial placement. The 100 children were all coming to those two provinces.

Our old log house was already bursting at the seams, and I told Bonnie I was apprehensive about the quality of our facilities here to receive a large number of boat children. She said, "Well, whatever they find here is better than the bottom of the ocean." When she gets in these terrible moods I don't like to argue with her.

As word of our need to expand our house spread, we received some help from the community. Some lumber was donated and a carpenter, bless his soul, donated a day or two, which was certainly a godsend, to rebuild the annex along the side of our house, stretching 20 feet out from the house wall and 45 feet long. But the expenses were more than the donations, and I asked her, "Where is the balance coming from, Bonnie?"

She said, "O, Fred. Don't always be worrying about money. If it's a good cause the money will be provided." The money was provided by joint bank account #3077-44.

In this same year, 1980, Mei-Lin developed a hearing problem which worried us. It was discovered that she had a perforated ear drum in her right ear. In March, 1980 it was replaced with a new ear drum. When she came home, two days later, she had a huge white bandage over the whole Eastern side of her head. She suffered some rude comments from her siblings until it was taken off two days later. Mei-Lin's ear healed and her hearing improved. Later the girls pierced their ears and wore multiple earrings around the rim of their ears.

Our nineteenth child arrived in August of 1980. KimChi was born in May, 1968 in Vietnam. When she was 11 years old she was babysitting for a well-to-do Chinese family in Vietnam. KimChi's father, a former police officer in the Saigon regime, had been jailed by the Communists when they took over.

When the Chinese family bought passage on a large boat, hoping to escape Vietnam, KimChi first told them she was going to stay in Vietnam, but then decided to go with them. She didn't have time to tell her parents. As she had no money for passage, she would travel as a stowaway. It was a large boat with many hundreds of people getting on. The boarding took place in the early evening of May 23rd, 1979. KimChi placed the toddler of the Chinese family on her shoulders, put her own coat around them both, and when the toddler's name was called, she went right on board in the evening twilight with the toddler. After the boat was underway, names were not checked again.

KimChi recently read a book by another woman who had escaped from Vietnam in a boat and said the passage below was a mirror of her own experience:

> "[In the boat] the small bulb hanging from a wire attached to a rusty nail spread a feeble, unchanging light. Deep inside the boat there was no distinction between day and night. The constant illumination protected us from the vastness of the sea and the sky all around us. The people sitting on the deck told us there was no boundary between the blue sky and the blue of the sea. No one knew if we were heading for the heavens or plunging into the water's depths. Heaven and hell embraced in the belly of our boat. Heaven promised a turning point in our lives, a new future, a new history. Hell, though, displayed our fears: fear of pirates, fear of starvation, fear of poisoning by biscuits soaked in motor oil, fear of running out of water, fear of being unable to stand up, fear of having to urinate in the red pot that was passed from hand to hand, fear that the scabies on the baby's head was contagious, fear of never again setting foot on solid ground, fear of never again seeing the faces of our parents." [24]

[24] Pp 3-4, **Ru,** by Kim Thuy, Bloomsbury, NY, 2012, quoted with permission

KimChi stayed on the boat for nine days and nights. The first land they saw was Malaysia, but they weren't welcomed there. People threw rocks at them. Finally the boat landed in Indonesia. The Chinese family told her it was because of them that she got her freedom. They wanted her to change her name and stay with them, presumably to babysit. But KimChi learned from some of the more knowledgeable young people on the boat that if she changed her name she would never be able to sponsor her family out of Vietnam. She decided to part from the Chinese family, quite a decision for an eleven-year-old girl.

KimChi then spent eight months in a camp in Indonesia for unaccompanied minor boat children. After she was accepted by Canadian Immigration officers who worked in the camp, KimChi was placed with a family in Quebec. It didn't work out, and in August, 1980 she arrived in our family. She spoke no English but she knew a little French, Viet Nam having been a French colony. Our kids were able to communicate with her in French which they were learning in school.

Sure enough, some boat children had difficulties at their original placement, so they came and crashed in with us temporarily, in twos and threes, about a dozen in all.

Vinh Hai was one of the boat children whose original placement in Canada didn't work out. His mother still lived in Vietnam. He stayed with us for the better part of a year. One of his first experiences at our place was to go with our kids on the school bus. At first Vinh Hai didn't catch the subtleties of English parlance. But he was a friendly fellow and would say, "Yeah, yeah" when anyone spoke to him. Some of his siblings took advantage of him and taught him a few of the more imaginative and cruder expressions in the English language. When the school bus stops at the railroad tracks, the rule is the kids all have to be quiet and listen for a train. But Vinh Hai, after some prodding, one time shouted something that included the "F" word during one of these stops, much to the mortification of old Mr McLeod, the driver.

Vinh Hai stayed with us for nine months

Mr McLeod took the bus across the tracks, slowly put on the hand brake and walked back to deal with this outrage. He looked Vinh Hai in the eye and said, "What are you, a wise guy?"

Vinh Hai (not understanding a word), with a smile said, "Yeah, yeah."

"I'm going to tell the principal on you - then you'll sing a different tune."

"Yeah, yeah."

Finally Shan saw that it had gone far enough and explained to Mr McLeod that Vinh Hai didn't understand English, and that he really was a good kid, which was true. Mr McLeod shook his head, walked back up front, and drove on. None of our kids will admit to complicity in this sordid affair.

Mei-Lin's and Tibiki's room was just over Vinh Hai's. His bed happened to be near the stovepipe going up through his room from the furnace below. One time a table knife dropped from Tibiki's dresser, hit the floor, bounced against the stovepipe and slid through down onto Vinh Hai, who had been resting peacefully. It just grazed his head. He let out a scream, accompanied with some colourful Vietnamese (we think) expletives.

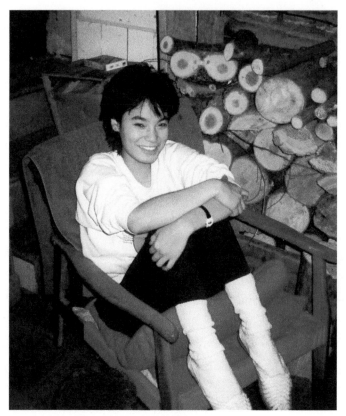

Tibiki, nice and warm by the wood stove

Tibiki rushed down to see what had happened and to retrieve the unintended weapon. She knocked on his door. When he opened it, he had already donned a hockey helmet for protection. He inquired, "WHAT YOU DOING?? YOU DINKEY DOW!! YOU CWAZY!!

186

YOU TRY KEEU ME!!" and gave her the table knife along with a piece of his mind, in vociferous Vietnamese.

Later I experienced existentially what is quaintly known as the language barrier. Vinh Hai and I were going to move some heavy cedar poles. As we picked up the first one, I had one end and he had the other. We were going to heave it onto a pile. I said: "At the count of three..."

While I was counting and bringing it back to heave, he actually heaved his end, which flew out, while the butt end I was holding came around and slammed into my cheekbone, knocking me dazed to the ground. Alarmed, he came quickly, and bending over me said, "Sorry! Sorry!" and was apologizing in Vietnamese. At least I think he was apologizing. I was sitting, still dazed for a while.

It wasn't his fault. The other kids, however, laughingly asked "Are you trying to 'keeu' Daddy?" He was feeling more and more guilty. When they saw how terribly distraught he was, they relented, and helped me explain to him that it was okay, and wasn't anyone's fault. Nevertheless, I had to go to the hospital in Alexandria and get three stitches. My cheekbone still hurts whenever I think about it.

In March, 1981, after being with us for nine months, Vinh Hai went to live with friends in Halifax, Nova Scotia. He got a job there on weekends washing dishes. Years before, when he was leaving Vietnam his mother gave him her only valuable possession - her wedding ring. She told him he could sell it if he was really down and out.

The evening before he went to Nova Scotia, Bonnie and I took Vinh Hai out to a restaurant for supper. As we talked, he said he wanted to do something special for Bonnie and she was quite moved to be given the gold wedding ring of his now deceased mother. He insisted she take it. Bonnie treasures it and still wears it next to the ring I gave her.

Chapter 21

Our Final Two Children – Really!!

Kalidas Nataraj George Cappuccino *arrived in 1981. Kalidas was a renowned third century A.D. Hindu poet, who wrote in Sanskrit. Nataraj is the lord of dance. George is Kalidas's given name.*

Tulsidas Ganesh Joseph Cappuccino *arrived in 1981. Tulsidas, the greatest of the Hindu poets, wrote the Ramayana, which was translated into English by Mahatma Gandhi. Ganesh is the popular elephant-headed god. Joseph is Tulsidas's given name.*

I want to point out to all and sundry that Bonnie had *pre-school* children in our family *for an uninterrupted period of 26 years,* until Vodinh started kindergarten. What a glorious day that was! No husband should have to endure such massive inconvenience and disruption.

I do try to be considerate. Some years ago when we had a 12-seater van and about ten school-age children plus several pre-schoolers, I thought with all those kids underfoot Bonnie really ought to have a vacation, lest she get burned out. I said to her, "Bonnie, you're getting burned out. You really need some relaxation. You need a little rest. Why don't I watch things here at the house, and you throw a few things into the van that you might need for a few days - Take the kids and go!" She never did take me up on that generous-hearted offer.

Annie Laurie and Mei-Lin

In November, 1981, Bonnie and Sandra, through FCC, brought to Canada 24 children, mostly babies, from our Bangladesh Home, for Canadian families. Among these children were also two special ones from our Podanur Home in India: two brothers, Kalidas, age ten, and Tulsidas, age eight, who arrived in Canada on Nov 22, 1981 and became part of our family. We had run out of names, so Bonnie found the name Kalidas, whose poem is in our Unitarian Hymnal, *Singing the Living Tradition:*

Look to this day!
For it is life, the very life of life...

189

For yesterday is but a dream,
And tomorrow is only a vision;
But today, well lived makes every yesterday
A dream of happiness.

A poem by Tulsi Das is found in *Hymns for the celebration of Life*, an earlier Unitarian Hymnal, #438 (before the protocol of degenderizing):

This and this alone is true religion –
To serve thy brethren.
In such a faith is happiness,

Kalidas, left, and Tulsidas when they first came to us

Tulsidas remembers being at a Christian Children's Home and having his hands struck with a cane frequently for childish misbehaviour. He ran away often. His grandmother didn't believe they were beating him but when he showed her the marks, she took him out of that place and brought him to *Families for Children* to be with his big brother, Kalidas.

One distinguishing characteristic of Tulsidas, even as an eight-year-old, was his deep bass voice. He always spoke with authority.

Kailash and Tulsidas

191

Vodinh and Tulsidas

Kalidas was a thoughtful child and never had much to say. He remembers being bitten on the ear by a monkey, and still bears the scar even unto this day. Sometimes the kids would write a letter to Santa Claus. In 1983 Kalidas wrote:

Dear Santa,
I would like for our Mom to stay home a lot more. We miss her when she goes to India. We love her very much.
Kalidas

**Top row, Tran, Kahlil, Shan, Ashok, Tibiki, KimChi, Mei-Lin, Mahleka.
Middle row, Kalidas, Bonnie, Fred, Shalini (who stayed with us for a while),
Shikha, Kailash, Bottom row, Vodinh and Tulsidas**

On January 19th, 1984 I took a day off to go with Bonnie for her appointment in Ottawa to have a cat-scan. About three months earlier, the hearing in her left ear faded to nothing. They thought it was caused by a virus. The cat-scan could not find anything amiss. All this did not affect her right ear, which was functioning normally. Years later we found that the hearing loss was due to a problem more serious than a virus. Meanwhile the kids gradually learned to talk into her right ear. When Bonnie and I would go somewhere in the car, she would do all the driving because that way her good ear was toward me. If we were mad at each other, I would drive.

In November, Ashok had an appendix operation. After the operation his stitches hurt when he laughed. This made it difficult when he was watching "Airplane," a comedy on TV, and the nurse had to come in and wheel him out of the TV room. The movie had him in stitches, and that hurt his stitches.

In looking at the family photos taken through the years, we noticed that during a certain period, Kailash often appeared glum and unsmiling. Around this time he developed a cough that persisted so we took him to a doctor who ordered X-rays which revealed a massive tumour in his chest. It had apparently been there since before he was born but hadn't shown up on previous X-rays. The doctors were decisive, and on Wednesday, March 6th, 1985, in a three-hour operation, removed the entire tumour, the size of two grapefruits. It had collapsed one lung and was pushing his heart against the other lung. After the operation Kailash had to endure chemotherapy and radiation.

For the radiation therapy Bonnie had to take him to Ottawa every day for four weeks. Our long-time friend, Vera Freud, *actually gave us her own car* for the two-hour round trip, a SAAB, with velvet seats and a seat warmer! It really helped to have a dependable car. The treatment caused Kailash to lose his hair, but he seemed to be doing quite well, with no trace of cancer.

He had to endure the trauma of losing his hair several times. Some years later we heard of a family in the same situation. The siblings of the cancer patient all shaved their heads in empathy and support. If only we had thought of that. Our kids would all have felt privileged to do that. Other kids at Glengarry District High School would likely have done the same.

Later, while in high school, Kailash got a job in the kitchen of a local truckers' restaurant off highway 417. He was washing pots and pans, but when there weren't enough cooks, it was discovered that he could fill this slot quite well. Kailash was doing fine until one trucker told the boss to "get rid of that Black guy in the kitchen." Kailash didn't hear anything about this from his boss, but some of his friends told him of this encounter.

The boss didn't fire Kailash, but neither did she give him the extra hours he had requested. I mentioned this to Professor Gary Geddes, our neighbour, and he called some friends who put together a letter to Kailash's boss which said in part:

Dear manager:

We hear that you have been put under pressure by a customer for your progressive hiring policy which encourages ethnic and visible minorities in the workplace. We want to congratulate you for rejecting outright such appalling racist attitudes and for making sure that the widest possible cross-section of members of our community is visible on all shifts in the restaurant and garage.

Sincerely,
Dr Gary Geddes, Writer and Professor
(and 13 other leading local citizens)

It was heartening to know that the community leaders supported our family and supported an open hiring policy. Finally Kailash quit the job for other reasons. Having overcome the threat of cancer and difficulties at his work place, Kailash seemed somewhat happier pursuing a career in the arts.

It was around 1988 that our friend Vera Freud called me from Paris: "Fred, send me some clippings about you and Bonnie – right away!" I knew if I didn't comply she would harass me terribly, so I sent off some stuff. Some weeks later a telegram arrived stating we had received an *Honourable Mention Award for the Teaching of Human Rights* from UNESCO (United Nations Education, Scientific and Cultural Organization). Honourable Mention usually means you didn't really win anything. I handed the telegram to Tulsidas to read. He looked at it and thought I had intended it to be put into the stove. He promptly did so. It was only later that we received word from UNESCO: "Are you coming to Paris to receive your award?" Apparently it was a big deal. We asked our friend Vera, who was in Paris at the time, to receive the award on our behalf, which she did. This award was a first for Canada.

Chapter 22

"Oh, My Son Absalom!" A Terrible Loss

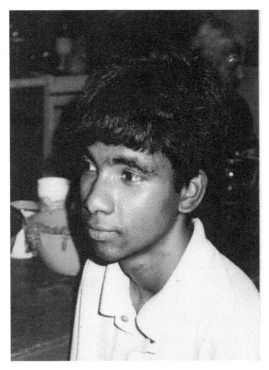

Kailash

We had Kailash for such a brief, precious time.

Many of our children have artistic talent, but they would all agree that Kailash was by far the most artistic of all. He did ink drawings and oil and water-colour paintings. He designed and made his own colourful clothes. He also had a free hair style, sometimes shaving half his head.

For several years, Kailash had been going through difficult times. It seems that he never fully recovered emotionally from the earlier (1985) surgery to remove the life-threatening tumour in his chest. The radiation and chemotherapy were particularly difficult for the child. He withdrew into himself.

The high school staff was superb. We consulted together and worried together about Kailash. They offered ideas and were ready to help in any way possible. He was repeatedly offered counselling with a psychologist. He refused.

His close friend, Mattias, committed suicide on April 15th, 1995. Kailash went into a deep despair from which he never recovered. Many of his friends called him often, trying to get through to him. Some called from Ottawa and some from Montreal but he wouldn't speak with them.

We tried to keep someone close to him at all times. He resented this and wanted to be left alone. So we relaxed our vigilance a little as we didn't want to arouse his resentment and precipitate something regrettable.

Tibiki and Kailash

Joan Auden, a social worker at the Ottawa Children's Hospital, knew Kailash well. She was also a close family friend. She suggested that a well-crafted letter to him might be useful. This was excellent advice. In the letter, we mainly told him we loved him. We know he read the letter because some of the wording was used in his last letters to family and friends..

On April 21st 1995, when we returned from a luncheon in Cornwall, we found Kailash had hanged himself in the basement. Bonnie screamed. It was the worse shock of our lives. I took him down immediately to look for a pulse. The first thing Bonnie did was call Dr Shah who said, "Oh Shit!" which somehow helped her. He had reacted as a close family friend, not as a distant professional. He asked if we had called the police and said we had to do that. Two police officers arrived. One said we should not have taken him down. Bonnie just looked at him in disbelief: How can you leave your child hanging? The policeman backed off on that point, and then interviewed all of us, respectfully taking copious notes.

Our minister, the Rev Brian Kopke of the Ottawa Unitarian Congregation, came to our house. We all sat in a circle while he took out his writing pad and said, "Tell me about Kailash." Each of us spoke many times. There was a lot of sober reminiscing, but a lot of laughter, too. The session lasted two hours and Brian took several pages of notes.

Kailash's suicide was the third from that school in a few months. The school staff was deeply worried about a possible epidemic of suicide and we discussed together how to stop the cycle.

The memorial service for Kailash's friend Mattias had been a private service. The traumatized family couldn't bear to include others. That was okay. We decided that our services should be open to any and all who knew Kailash. The school staff expressed deep appreciation for our decision to do this as many of the students needed this kind of focus for mourning and reflecting.

One of Kailash's many paintings

Brian did two services, one at our Unitarian Church in Ottawa, and one in Alexandria at the United Church which was generously offered to us. All were invited. Classes were suspended for the duration and many students and teachers attended. The two services were filled to overflowing. Both included a time for people in the congregation to share thoughts about Kailash. This proved to be a healing time especially for the students in Alexandria.

Many people came up to talk to us. We learned that Kailash had been generous with his paintings. They were all over the community. One stranger said, "O, yes, I have one of his drawings. I framed it for the family room."

We found Naomi Bronstein's name in the guest book. She had driven an hour and a half from Montreal, but apparently was too choked up to talk with us.

A third service, an informal tree-planting on our farm, was held with family and a few close friends. Our son Pierre took the initiative by announcing to all his siblings, "Everybody has to be present at the tree planting. You don't have to say anything if you don't want to, but everybody has to be there." Pierre sensed that some may have been wondering if they had the energy to go through another service. But if they didn't they might regret it later. I think they all really did want to be a part of this final farewell to their brother.

We gathered in a circle and planted a tree – a black cherry. Each of us, including our small grandchildren, had the opportunity to say a few words about Kailash and to scatter a spoonful of his ashes. Most of us said a few words. A few, unable to speak, just spread some ashes. Of all the words spoken, Bonnie's struck me the most intensely. Having been in kind of a daze up to this point, I hadn't been moved to tears until then. Bonnie said, "It is not right for parents to bury their children. The children should bury the parents." I held her close and we wept together profusely. Our twenty children gathered round and held us both. It was the most meaningful service of all.

In hindsight, we think Kailash may have been gay. If we had realized that earlier, perhaps we could have saved him.

Life goes on.

"O my son Absalom, my son, my son Absalom! would God I had died for thee, O Absalom, my son, my son!" [25]

---

[25] King David mourning his son, in Second Samuel 18:33, King James Version.

Chapter 23

Farmstead Anecdotes

One of the great morale builders in a family is doing something strenuous and meaningful together. Our tractor, for no reason, would develop mud sickness and pick the remotest parts of the woods when it chose to do so. We used to get poles and chains, and spend hours trying to lever it out. When we had only eight kids at home, we heaved and pulled, and some even swore - but we couldn't budge it. Humiliated, we'd call our neighbour Johnny Stewart, to come over with his tractor and haul us out.

Later on, when we had 16 kids at home, we dragged a 30-foot cable out there, hooked it on to the front of the embedded tractor, and 32 hands grabbed aholt. Kalidas started up the tractor's diesel engine to get the big wheels slowly moving in the mud, and at the signal we all strained and groaned, pulling on the cable. Slowly, slowly, the monster inched forward, out of the mud onto firmer ground. Up rose a spontaneous "YEAAAAY!!!" from 16 kids and their old man. 16 kids are exactly 1.27 horsepower. If you add the old man, it's 1.28 hsp. We have to be scientific about these things.

Mohan, Robin, Pierre, Fred, Tran, Kahlil. I'd give two bits to know what Pierre is whispering to Mohan

One evening Tran was trying to get the little electric chain saw going. It's a lot less noisy than the gas ones. The motor was humming, but Tran couldn't get it to cut at all. Tran insisted that I sharpen it. He said he and Shan had both sharpened it and it was still dull. So I got the file and sharpened it again. Then I took it out and tried it. Terrible. I had never seen such a dull saw. It just didn't cut at all. Then I remembered that someone had taken off the chain for some reason. All of a sudden it became clear. I said to Tran, "I know what's wrong with this saw."

At that point Tran also had the insight: "Daddy, the chain is on backwards."

Kahlil piling firewood for cutting later on

Another time, Johnny Simpson came running into the house: "MICHAEL'S PINNED UNDER THE TRACTOR!!"

"WHERE?"

"WAY BACK IN THE WOODS!"

"IS HE HURT BADLY?"

"I DON'T KNOW!"

"IS HE MAKING ANY NOISE?"

"IS HE EVER - HE'S SCREAMING HIS HEAD OFF!" So we knew he was alive at least.

Thinking that the tractor might be crushing the life out of him, I ran with the other kids, while Bonnie called an ambulance and the neighbours.

Both were quick to respond.

When we got to him, I was immensely relieved to see that it was only his foot that was pinned. The sequence of events was one that takes place all too often with farm tractors. Michael had been pulling a log with a chain, but the chain was attached too high up on the tractor - above the level of the axle - so when the log jammed against some trees, it stopped abruptly. But the tractor wheels kept moving forward and pulling against the chain, so that the front end of the tractor rose up and somersaulted over backwards.

Michael had the amazing good sense and agility to jump sideways, or he would have been killed instantly. But the tractor fender caught his foot.

Terry Sweitzer, a nurse, rushed in from Dunvegan, three miles away. She had a bundle of sanitary napkins, and explained that it was good for controlling heavy bleeding. She used it as padding to try to cushion Michael's leg. He recalls wondering later what all the sanitary napkins were doing out there in the woods.

Finally, Huey MacLennan (John Archie's son) arrived with a jack and slowly jacked up the tractor so Michael could be moved out carefully and placed on a blanket over two ironwood poles. Four guys ran with him to the ambulance parked near the house. Bonnie went with Michael in the ambulance. Both bones in Michael's leg were broken above the ankle and a cast was put on his leg which reached up to the middle of his thigh.

We immediately installed a roll bar on the tractor for $1000. When Michael came home after two weeks in the hospital, he was able, even with his cast on, to drive his car. Lucky for him - and for the rest of us. He's not very good at bed rest.

John Archie told us later, "I was sure Michael was a goner when I heard the tractor had flipped over on him. He's one lucky boy."

Years earlier one of the kids suggested that since the bull calves were going to be eaten, we should name them appropriately. They became "Whopper," "Pizza," "Big Mac," and then we had one named "No Potatoes." [26]

Our Holstein, Matilda (from *Waltzing Matilda)* had a heifer calf that was sired by Whopper, a Jersey. We didn't know Whopper was old enough at eleven months, but he did breed the cow. This was a big relief to us because the artificial breeding sometimes involved several attempts, a month apart.

One day Whopper got into the garden and trampled some Swiss chard and some little cucumber plants. When Bonnie tried to shoo him out, he put his head down and started to paw the ground. One does not paw the ground in front of Bonnie when one is a bull calf. As a farm girl, she knew it was the auspicious hour - according to the juxtaposition of moon and planets - to summon the abattoir. Poor Whopper went to his Heavenly Reward. Our earthly reward was steaks for the freezer. The kids all loved Whopper, both as an individual and as steaks.

Bonnie sometimes made a cheese from one morning's milk from Betsy, using about two gallons. Betsy gave another two at night. The finished cheese weighed two to three pounds. To produce the best taste the cheese should be aged for six months but we were lucky if it lasted six hours. The kids used it for toasted cheese sandwiches.

All in all, the cows were a big plus. Since we had to maintain the tractor to plow the lane and to bring in firewood, baling hay enough for several cows didn't cost very much. We were in milk all year. If there is a surplus of one commodity from which a big family can benefit, it is milk. From the milk we made butter, cheese and yoghurt. We had paid $500 for Matilda. She contributed five gallons a day and at retail prices, five gallons would have cost $10 back then. With her milk she paid for herself in 50 days, and gave us a calf as well. The cows were a huge economic benefit.

[26] "All that Meat and No Potatoes" - Louis Armstrong.

KimChi was one of our best milkers. She got attached to Chantal, and when it was time to send her to the abattoir (Chantal, not KimChi) she decided she (KimChi, not Chantal) would be vegetarian, at least as far as Chantal was concerned.

Chantal was the biggest cow we ever had. She gave lots of milk, but she was a bony old creature. One summer Tibiki was trying to teach Chantal how to be an ox and pull things in case we needed to go into the bush in winter for firewood. The firewood was unreachable for many months in winter with the tractor because of tractor-gobbling snow drifts.

Tibiki rigged up a harness for Chantal using baler twine and a horse collar. The horse collar can be worn upside down on a cow. John Archie had taught us that. The baler twine was doubled, and then attached to both ends of a whiffle-tree she found in a shed. The centre of the whiffle-tree was attached with more baler twine to the sledge. The sledge was a forked cedar tree we had specially cut, with the stump curved up, and the two branches dragging like a sled.

Tibiki got Chantal all connected, and then Chantal wouldn't move. So Tibiki put some grain in the grain bucket and that got the cow moving. But after she started, she realized something was dragging behind. It's a good thing we had her in the fenced pasture, because she took off, galloping three times around the corral, as fast as she could, banging the sledge against boulders and fences, and almost killing herself. Then she stopped, puffing. It's a wonder she didn't have a coronary. After that episode, Tibiki decided Chantal was too stupid to be an ox.

Our log house, painted by Kalidas

For a time we had nine Cappuccino kids at Glengarry District High School. Our whole family was clothed from the garbage bags full of hand-me-down clothes given to me by the nurses at Macdonell Memorial Hospital in Cornwall where I worked. We hardly ever bought any clothes, shoes, boots, etc. KimChi told me, "The kids at school think we're rich. They ask where we bought the clothes, and we tell them it's all from garbage bags, and they don't believe us." A few of our older kids started working and buying some of their own clothes, which looked almost as good as the ones from the garbage bags.

On school mornings, the 16 kids would walk down our lane to the school bus, usually in the same order, with Pierre last, hollering, "Hold the bus! I'm coming!" On some days there was a neighbour's car parked down the road with relatives from Edmonton or Winnipeg, silently watching. Apparently our mixed-culture children were a tourist attraction.

While she was in high school KimChi got a week-end job in Alexandria as a house-person in a group home with six mentally disabled men. She did well, organizing the cooking, cleaning, and getting them to do things for themselves. An industrious child, she later managed to repay her airfare to the Canadian government, and she sent money to her parents in Vietnam. She never paid me for all the expense entailed in her living with us. But, Bonnie was not help at all. Bonnie told her, "KimChi, I am so proud of you."

After the kids grew up, I learned about some of the things they did when I was not with them. Sometimes when they were out cutting trees in the woods, if a tree got hung up on another tree, one or two of them would climb up high in the tree and shake it back and forth until it came loose. Then they would hang on as the tree came crashing down - WHOOSH! How any of them survived is a mystery.

When we put the tin roof on the annex alongside the house, I invested in half a dozen hammers. I thought, with all those kids, we might as well get some return, so they all helped to nail the roof on. That was going fairly well until I noticed one kid was pounding in nails, 16.3% of which were bent over, nevertheless being pounded in.

Those hammers weren't such a good investment after all, because the roof leaked like a sieve. So I made a second investment of half a dozen buckets. Every time it rained one of the kids asked me, "Dad, when are we going to fix the roof?"

But things have to wait their turn, and I said, "Well, we'll fix the roof when our ship comes in."

I guess I kept saying that, and Kalidas finally announced, "Daddy, your ship is at the bottom of the ocean."

The kids had acquired a little rubber dinghy one year which they used on our pond, Loch Haven, but through the winter it got many holes in it. The next spring I was dragging it to the van to take to the dump when Tulsidas, coming out of the house, hollered, "Hey, guys! Look at Dad! His ship came in!"

Our greenhouse was made from perfectly bent cedar poles cut from our woods, and scrounged windows. It opened to the outside, left, and also to the Annex inside. Kalidas is watching Robin at the chain saw. With some anguish, we reluctantly decided not to submit this photo to *House Beautiful* magazine

210

Chapter 24

Anecdotes from Later Years

Bonnie had a motto on her fridge: "Insanity is hereditary - you get it from your children." Sometimes also, one gets a sense of perspective from one's children. Our first-born son, Robin Hood, like his parents, considers himself to be a Gandhian. He has long been dedicated to the cause of justice and world peace. Some years ago he and a group of demonstrators protested against the launching of a Trident nuclear submarine in Groton, Connecticut. The Trident has dozens of rockets, each with a nuclear warhead. One submarine has the potential to obliterate an entire continent. But there is a lot of money to be made in arms-manufacturing, so the insanity continues.

A big party was being thrown by the industry (invitation only) to celebrate the launch. Robin said, "The invitations for my friends and me must have got lost in the mail." They went anyhow, and courted arrest by kneeling in front of the entrance gates where people were going in to party. The kneelers were arrested. In the jailhouse they decided to fast. Years earlier, Mahatma Gandhi fasted, sometimes for 30 days, but Gandhi did take water. Because of the urgency of the issue, Robin and a few friends decided to refuse water as well as food. The human body can safely endure about four days of this punishment. After that there is danger to kidneys and other organs.

"Several days into our fast the guards loaded us into wheel-chairs and took great delight in wheeling us past the cafeteria window with a big hamburger on display. They didn't realize that I was a vegetarian. I do have to admit, though, that hamburger did look pretty good. Finally on the fifth day, the prison warden said, 'I have spoken with the authorities, and they all agreed that if you were to stay in prison you'd be force-fed intravenously. That would cost $500 a day, and you guys just aren't worth it.' So they let us go."

Late in 1988 someone told me they saw Robin on TV. He and some of his friends organized a demonstration in Vermont against the Gatling gun made by General Electric. The gun shoots 6000 rounds of ammunition a minute. The El Salvador Government used these guns in helicopters to "pacify" villages that were suspected of causing trouble. In a few seconds the village was levelled and all living creatures including children were obliterated.

Before the demonstration Robin and a few friends went to the Vermont National Guard and explained that the demonstration was not against them, and that the group was planning to go onto the testing ground of these weapons and set up a cardboard village. Robin was pleased that the National Guard took a neutral stance regarding the demonstration.

In 1968 we had purchased 17 acres from our Unitarian friends who owned about a square mile of forest in Vermont. Right after high school Robin went to live there and has been there ever since. When he first moved there, he noticed one morning that the beavers had started building a dam right in the middle of the road. He moved all the branches off the road to a line about eight feet away from the road. The next morning the beavers had moved everything back to the middle of the road. Robin moved it all back again eight feet away. Next morning same thing occurred. Robin consulted the township. The guy said they would have to trap and shoot the beavers.

Robin said, "Let me try a little longer." He moved the branches off again, and this time piled big rocks on top of them. The beavers started building their dam in the proper place, and a few days later the completed dam was three feet above the road level, and safely eight feet away from the road.

Today, the whole acreage, about a square mile of forest, including our 17 acres, has been formed into a not-for-profit Land Trust called Wheelock Mountain Farm. Robin often hosts workshops on environmental, peace, and human rights issues. When Robin is not travelling overseas with his mother, he is working on these issues.

In 1975 the war in Vietnam ended. KimChi's father was released from prison a few months later. As soon as the government opened the door for foreigners in 1989, KimChi and her fiancé, Nam, went back to Vietnam for a visit. In the village where Nam's father lived, KimChi and Nam were married in the happy presence of both families. [27]   Many in the village were communists and their high-ranking officials had to be invited to the wedding. KimChi's father was introduced to the gathering as a businessman, and no mention was made of his past as a policeman.

**Nam's and KimChi's wedding reception included Nam's nephews and nieces.
The girl smiling at right is Anne Quach**

[27] KimChi's niece, on her husband's side, is Anne Quach. In 2015 Anne was re-elected as a Member of Parliament for the Riding of Beauharnois-Salaberry, Quebec, one of two Vietnamese-Canadian MPs. New Democratic Party, of course.

Anne Quach was re-elected in (2015) as a Member of Parliament

KimChi and Nam were married a second time a few months later in Montreal with myself officiating. During the wedding and reception, as per Vietnamese tradition, she changed from her white dress to a bright red one, and again to a bright yellow one.

A few years later when she came home for a visit, KimChi and Nam brought their first-born daughter with them. She handed her baby to Mohan but the baby cried. As she took her baby back, KimChi comforted Mohan saying, "She's afraid of ugly."

KimChi and her daughter who "is afraid of ugly"

In 1995 Shan found in an old cookbook a letter Pierre had written 21 years earlier. Pierre was 16 at the time. The envelope was postmarked "Toronto, April 1, 1974." We can't remember the circumstances, but the letter in its entirety stated:

Dear Mom,
I am in Toronto now and had a great trip. Next time I leave don't get so
hysterical.
With love, Pierre

One time, when Tibiki's first daughter, Ashley, was two years old she was greeted by a stranger in a store who bent down and asked her, "And who is the most beautiful girl in the world?"

Easy question for Ashley. She pointed and replied, "Mommy."

Tibiki at the grand entrance of our log mansion.
The door was scrounged from the local dump

Our children went to elementary school in Maxville. While in high school, Kahlil became totally immersed in the drum section, playing the big bass drum. The village was also home to the Glengarry Pipe Band which he joined, and through the years he travelled many places with them, often visiting Scotland. The band won many awards, as did Kahlil individually. In 2004 he won *Best Bass Drum* at the World Pipe Band Championships held in Glasgow, Scotland with Grade 2 bands. In 2009 in Halifax, Nova Scotia, he also played in concert with Paul McCartney from the Beatles. Kahlil never tells his parents about these things. Friends from Victoria inform us.

Bonnie got a sari to wear at the Scottish Highland Games in Maxville with the Cappuccino (?) tartan. Kahlil's drum set the pace for the Pipe Band

Buckminster Fuller, one of the great innovative minds of our time, was known for his interest in world problems and improving human lives. In his acceptance speech on being named Humanist of the Year by the

American Humanist Association in 1969, he said something that resonated with Bonnie:

With the birth of our second child, I found myself doing the first really good thinking, thinking on my own, that I have ever done. It was a fantastic responsibility, a new life coming to us. I said if this new child were to be the kind of child I hoped she would be, she would become very unhappy if, as she grew older, she found I devoted myself to trying to bring advantage to her, then found herself in a world where there was great disadvantage for others. But on the other hand, she would be extremely happy if she discovered as she grew up that I had committed myself, not merely to solving problems for her, but I had committed myself to the attempt to solve humanity's problems.

Chapter 25

The Forming of Child Haven

Years ago a research article in *Psychology Today* regarding the birth order of siblings stated that *the older sister of brothers, when she grows up, can handle any number of children.* Bonnie had two younger brothers. She later raised 21 children without having a nervous breakdown. Her husband had 21 nervous breakdowns.

It was in 1985 that Bonnie and I left *Families for Children* to start a new organization called *Child Haven International* [28] - less Canadian-oriented and more Gandhian-oriented. Around this time a television crew came to film a program on our family. [29] We routinely refused these offers, but the producer was willing to promote our new endeavour, *Child Haven*, so we agreed. The cameras were in our kitchen during supper. KimChi, sitting next to me, had her entire pork chop balanced on a fork, heartily devouring big bites. I whispered, "Use your knife!" She looked at me quizzically. I repeated, "Use your knife!" Finally she got the message, put the chop back on her plate and started using her knife and fork. Just at that moment, on the other side of the room, the camera was honing in on Tulsidas, with a bigger pork chop balanced precariously on his fork, gnawing away with primeval relish. To make the shot more exciting, he

[28] www.childhaven.ca
[29] *Country Report*, with Wayne Rostad

commenced to lick the gravy from his knife. The dramatic results of our child rearing were immortalized on television.

Dr Nat Shah, our family doctor, agreed to be a board member for *Child Haven* along with Peter Freud. Our first location for a children's home was at a hospital Dr Shah was instrumental in building in Dhanera Village, North Gujarat. Our son Mohan was involved in this first successful establishment of a Home. He left his studies at McGill and went to Dhanera, India, for a three-month term. He ran the Home and at one time had seven children there. Because *Child Haven* was very new we were unable to send a replacement for him immediately. After Mohan's three months were up he sent us frantic letters: "Please send a volunteer to replace me so I can come home and go back to university!" Mail from India back then often took four weeks. Mohan had to remain there for nine months before a replacement arrived, after which time he returned to McGill and finished his degree in Anthropology.

From that beginning *Child Haven* expanded to include nine Children's Homes caring for 1300 formerly destitute children. There are now six Homes in India and one each in Bangladesh, Nepal, and Tibet in China. (The Chinese Ambassador's wife suggested we add "in China" wherever we mention Tibet). At this writing Bonnie goes overseas four times a year (6½ weeks each time) to administer the Homes.

We also support financially a few children in Afghanistan and Bhutan.

Child Haven **does not do adoptions,** mainly because most of the children in our Homes have some family who are unable to raise them.

Looking east at our house in about 1990. The addition at right houses *Child Haven* headquarters. It was built with a gift from the late Morse Saito to Bonnie and me. Morse's Japanese-American family, even though they were American citizens, were interned during World War II. Morse later received $20,000 in reparation money from the U. S. Government. He gave us the entire amount, saying "It's not for Child Haven – it's for you." Bonnie thought the best gift for her was to get *Child Haven* out of her log house kitchen.

Our house in 2005. The left and middle sections are the siding-covered log house. At left, a 20-foot extension of the house toward the camera was made possible by a bequest from Fred's Aunt Alice

221

Chapter 26

Horns of a Dilemma

In June 1985 Bonnie returned from her first *Child Haven* trip to India on a huge Air India plane. The plane flew from India to Toronto where some passengers got off and some got on. It was in Toronto that a bomb was placed on board. Bonnie was on the plane with the bomb from Toronto to Montreal where she disembarked. The plane took off again but never reached its destination back to India. The bomb exploded in the hold, and the plane crashed into the Atlantic Ocean near Ireland.

While I was waiting for her in Montreal, I noticed an older couple at the ticket counter trying to get two seats together in the non-smoking section. They were told there were seats but none together. They chose to be together in the smoking section. They died together when the plane went down in the Irish Sea.

Bonnie and I were shaken for several days. Bonnie refused to be intimidated. She would continue going to India.

I suggested maybe Bonnie should do what Lotta Hitchmanova did when she was running the Unitarian Service Committee of Canada. Lotta got herself a uniform so she would be recognizable to the public. At the end of one of Bonnie's trips she showed up at the airport decked out in an Indian sari with 14 bracelets on her arms and 40 cultural medallions around her neck. She had gathered them from Bangladesh, Nepal, and India and they are a form of revelry in a sometimes dreary world. They are also a way of identifying with the local people. Bonnie is very frugal and these ornaments are inexpensive. Regarding her cultural jewellery, St Paul said that wives should be subject to their husbands. Among all those medallions she is wearing, not one has any connection to St Paul.

Now she wears beautiful hand-me-down saris every day, some of them given to her by her Ismaili friend, Naseem Vellani in Toronto, a follower of His Holiness the Aga Khan. Naseem gathers used saris from her many Ismaili friends. Regardless of all her other duties, Bonnie takes 26.4 minutes every morning to put on her sari. She knows her husband has a weakness for a woman in a sari, especially her.

In her short life of 81 years, Bonnie has had two life-threatening operations. The first was around 1990 when she fainted in a department store and fell to the floor, scaring the life out of Vodinh who was with her. Dr Shah immediately arranged for hospital tests, which eventually showed a brain tumour. It was removed. Luckily it was benign, an acoustic neuroma on the acoustic nerve and involving the facial nerve. That side of her face became paralysed because the facial nerve had to be cut to remove the tumour. A small gold weight was implanted into her left eyelid so that her eye would close better. She still has to put drops into her eye several times a day to keep it from drying out.

The second operation was around 2009. From a blood test Dr Shah knew something was wrong and immediately had her take an intestinal scope, which found a tumour. He again arranged surgery, removing all of the cancer and a foot of her colon, saving her life a second time. She is not impressed when I call her "My Sweet Semi-colon." In celebrating her 81st birthday she said, "It's so sad – half my life is gone already."

The point of relating all this is to report that – even with the inconvenience and discomfort of having to administer eye drops several times a day before the dryness starts to hurt – she has never, ever complained or felt sorry for herself. Although once she did holler at me, "Fred, stop rushing me when I'm putting drops in my eye." I did.

When she returns from visiting the *Child Haven* Homes overseas and gets off the plane, I never know what to expect. One time she got off the plane at Mirabel airport, and she had a big smile - and a little gold knob stuck through her nostril.

Another time she got off the plane, and she had a big smile – and she announced that henceforth she and I were vegetarians.

Another time she got off the plane, and she had a big smile and I gave her a hug, and we walked along pushing the luggage carts. She was all decked out in a sari, with all those bracelets and medallions jangling along in the airport like a walking Christmas tree. She glanced over at me and said, "Fred, straighten your tie. Can't you see all those people looking at you?"

To get a few minutes alone with her, what I have to do sometimes, with all the kids and confusion at home, is to take her out to a restaurant. There's one in Cornwall where we go - it has the style to which we have become accustomed. It's the truckers' place along the 401.

She was in the ladies' washroom there one evening, wearing her sari and all her paraphernalia and a young woman came up mystified and cautiously asked Bonnie, "Do you speak English?"

Bonnie said, "Yes."

"Where do you come from?"

"I'm Canadian."

"Where did you get all that jewellery?"

"Oh, it came from many different places, and it's all quite inexpensive."

And the girl looked her over and said, "Do you ever take them off?"

"No, I don't".

And I can personally attest to that. One night I was sleeping peacefully, and I guess a mosquito was hovering near my head. Kerrash! - a locomotive slammed into my ear. While the wheels were still clanging, I heard the mosquito buzzing off to safer quarters.

With all that jewellery jangling, Bonnie has some notable experiences. A friend told me he was walking along Second Street in Cornwall, and heard a car smash into the one in front of it. Then he noticed Bonnie sauntering along the sidewalk on the other side of the street. The driver had become momentarily entranced with a vision in a sari, bracelets, and bangles and didn't see the line of traffic stop in front of him.

After the crash, Bonnie kept striding down the sidewalk. She's deaf on that side, so she was smiling, blissfully unaware of anything amiss. I'm married to a traffic hazard.

Another day Bonnie and I were walking in Cornwall near the scrap metal yard with the wooden fence. I told her not to get too close, in case they turned on the big crane with the electro-magnet. But Bonnie is stubborn and said, "I have a right to walk on this street." Just then the magnet turned on, and Bonnie's bracelets and necklaces slammed her against the wood fence. I had all I could do to pry her loose. Bonnie doesn't remember it at all. She says I dreamed this one.

So I'm on the horns of a dilemma: On the one hand, I try to escape, because what the future holds for me is certainly either the madhouse or the poorhouse. But on the other hand, in spite of everything, I still get weak in the knees when I look at her. So that's the dilemma I'm in.

WHERE ARE THEY IN 2015?

(in order of their joining the family)

Robin Hood Cappuccino: Gandhian Peace and Justice Activist in Vermont, Director of *Child Haven* USA

Machiko Cappuccino: Housekeeping Supervisor in a hotel, Washington, D.C.

William Tell Cappuccino: Semi-retired high school teacher, Texas

Pierre Ceresole Cappuccino: Logistics for U.S. Navy, Seattle

Annie Laurie Cappuccino: Director of Admission, Science Recruitment, Brown University, Rhode Island

Michael Scott Cappuccino: IT Manager at a Customer Contact Center for a major hotel chain, Ontario

Mohanlal Ananda Cappuccino: Manager of Customer Service Operations at a Real Estate College in Toronto

Tran Thai Tong Cappuccino: On-Line Sales, Alexandria, Ontario

Kahlil Berrigan Cappuccino: Administrative position with the Canadian Government, Ottawa

Shikha Deepa Margaret Cappuccino: Data-entry expert, Ottawa

Lakshmi Bic Nellie McClung McRae: Nurse in Texas

Tibiki Nimki Jane Eyre Cappuccino: Homemaker, part-time caterer, Ontario

Vodinh Nhat Hanh Cappuccino: Construction/Driver, Ottawa

Ashok Vijayakumar Cappuccino: Truck driver, Ottawa

Kailash Shantidas Tagore Cappuccino: (deceased – April 21, 1995)

Mahleka Kwelanga Uhuru Cappuccino: Cook/Support Worker, Ottawa

Mei-Lin Yin Yee Cappuccino: Community Health Worker, British Columbia

Shan Ho Yin Cappuccino: Realtor, Ottawa

KimChi Tran: Homemaker, Montreal

Kalidas Nataraj George Cappuccino: Chef, Ottawa

Tulsidas Ganesh Joseph Cappuccino: Owner, Fresh Fish Shop, Ottawa

A Final Word from Bonnie and Fred

Glowing

Glowing deep - within each one of you - is a divine spark.

Though some of you may be skeptical, or feel you are unworthy - yet the divine spark glows - there inside you.

Sometimes it is overlaid with self-interest; sometimes it is encrusted with fear - yet the divine spark illumines your soul.

We may tend to deny it - knowing that we have done those things which we ought not to have done. Yet the divine spark never leaves you.

Jesus said the same in his own idiom: the Kingdom of God is within you.

This divine spark may surprise you as the future unfolds. It may lead you to risk much in some wild act of compassion.

You are of infinite worth; you possess a dazzling beauty that is irresistible. Trust this divine spark glowing –

Glowing in your deepest being. FC, 2005

Sketch of Bonnie and Fred by Andrina Cox

Now in it's second printing, the long awaited and universally acclaimed book

BONNIE AND HER 21 CHILDREN
by Fred Cappuccino, JBS*, her longsuffering husband
Published by Bonnie Books

(___)   1 Book @ $ 25 (tax & shipping included)
(___)   4 Books @ $ 90 (tax & shipping included) (one address only)
(___)5-9Books @ $ 22 each book (tax & shipping included)(one address)
(___) 10 Books @ $200 (tax & shipping included)(one address only)

Bulk orders, pricing available upon request (call 613-527-2829)
Your best deal: 100,000 books @ $1,400,000 (only $14 per book!)

Order through my web site:
www.BonnieAndHer21Children.com
or send cheque payable to "Bonnie Books Inc."

For Canadian orders: P.O. Box 1304
                              Alexandria, ON
                              K0C 1A0

For USA orders: PO Box 88, Greensboro Bend, Vermont 05842

Name_____

Address_____

Phone_____e-mail _____

A generous portion of the profits will go to Child Haven International

*Just Barely Surviving